GOLF:
BETTER PRACTICE FOR BETTER PLAY

By
Linda K. Bunker, Ph.D.
and
DeDe Owens, Ed.D.

Leisure Press
Champaign, IL

Library of Congress Catalog Card Number 83-80712

ISBN 0-88011-181-X

Printed in the United States of America

10   9   8   7   6   5

Leisure Press
A Division of Human Kinetics Publishers, Inc.
Box 5076, Champaign, IL 61825-5076
1-800-747-4457

CONTENTS

ACKNOWLEDGMENTS

This book would not have been possible without the joint efforts of many friends and colleagues who willingly gave their time and assistance. It is impossible to individually name each person who provided support. Please know that we thank each of you.

We would like to extend our special thanks to Sarah Odom for patience and assistance with the editing and typing of the manuscript. Additional editorial thanks are extended to Dick Taylor and Betty E. Morrison. We would like to express our appreciation to Linda Pratter (technique section) and Jan Marr (equipment) for their photographic contributions, David Whitfield for demonstrating the techniques, and Strictly Golf for the use of the equipment in the photographs. Special thanks are extended to Carol Davis and Barbie Bancroft for their illustrations in the chapter on Laws, Principles, and Preferences. In addition, we would like to thank those individuals who contributed specific informational input: Carol Johnson, advanced short game techniques; Garry Ross, alternatives for conditioning; and Dave Rowlands and Doug Sherman, use of their Rules Test.

We would also like to thank the National Golf Foundation and the many teachers and coaches throughout the country for providing us an opportunity to share and learn from interested students of the game. Those who are particularly interested in golf and who desire to grow personally in their games to expand their knowledge and to share their enthusiasm for the game with others are the ones to whom we dedicate this book.

There are those who dream and keep their dreams to themselves. And there are those who have their dreams come true by sharing those dreams with others.

Linda K. Bunker, Ph.D.

DeDe Owens, Ed. D.

Figure 1.1. Searching for the perfect swing.

1

INTRODUCTION

The game of golf is a very complex and intriguing one. The fact that you are reading this book indicates that you have already conquered some of the specific challenges of golf, or at least that you are interested in a victory over them. You may already be a proficient golfer, looking merely to improve your game. Or you may be a beginner seeking to understand the idiosyncrasies of this complex sport. In either case, you will find some of the answers to your questions in this book.

You have probably already experienced the exhilaration and frustration of hitting slices and hooks. There is nothing more rewarding than hitting a slice when you want to — nor more frustrating than hitting one when it is not desired. The beauty is that you can learn to control it in both conditions.

You can learn to control the physical aspects of your golf game. You can also learn to control the mental aspects. If you have spent the "sweat equity" hitting thousands of golf balls to acquire a good golf swing, you can also learn to control your mind so that your swing can run off when desired.

When you look over a golf hole, do you see yourself hitting a perfect drive? Or do you see your ball landing in a bunker or going out of bounds? You must learn to control your mind as well as your body.

You must learn to hit a slice when you want to. Or to hit a hook when you want to. After all, what other sport attempts to rehabilitate both a hooker and a pusher! And to provide all the necessary skills through personal dedication.

There is a wonderful story from Zigler's *See You at the Top* (see References) about a golfer who had obviously practiced his game rather hard and that story provides a good introduction to this book:

Major Nesmeth was a weekend golfer who often shot in the 90s. Then he quit for seven years, and the next time he played he shot a 74. What happened in between?

During those seven years, Major Nesmeth took a vacation from golf, but not from life. During that time, he spent his days in a 4½-foot X 5-foot cell, as a POW in Vietnam. His story is a great illustration of the principle that we must invest in the reaching, see the reaching, if we are to "reach the reaching."

Major Nesmeth was held in isolation for the first five years. He saw no one, and spoke to no one but himself. But he realized that survival would be dependent upon his doing something, so he chose golf! And he played golf every day — in his mind.

He saw himself hit golf balls, dress for competition, take time to set up, swing, and evaluate each shot. He did everything perfectly. It took him a full 4½ hours to play the course each time.

And when he really played the course, it took 4½ hours, and he shot a 74! He was able to capitalize upon his mental powers, and combine them with his physical skills.

Fortunately for us, we can actually practice our physical skills, and then optimize them with positive mental skills. This book will help you do just that. It will:
- Emphasize good mechanics of a golf swing.
- Illustrate practice techniques for improved performance.
- Teach mental skills to optimize potential.

The nature of golf requires a certain amount of compassion for the game, and obstinacy for its challenges. If you can recognize your own skills and learn to be objective about their application you can become a good golfer. If you wish to be serious about your practice, you can become a better golfer.

This book has three major objectives. The first objective is to help you identify more efficient ways to practice. These techniques will focus on effective practice drills and the information that they should convey. They will also help you plan your practice sessions so that you can optimize the time spent and capitalize on the improvements made.

Translating the improvements you make in practice to improved scores in your rounds of golf is the second objective of this book. It will help you see your practice pay off in lowered scores on the course. You will attain a new sense of confidence, and new skills to demonstrate on the course.

The third objective is to help you learn to "manage" your round of golf. You will be better able to identify your own strengths and weaknesses and capitalize on those of the golf course. You will learn to save strokes by analyzing each golf hole, and by plotting a strategy to capitalize on your strengths.

"Better Play Through Better Practice" will become your motto. As you recognize the benefit of systematic practice, you will realize the effects through lower scores.

SEARCHING FOR THE PERFECT SWING

The game of golf is certainly an intriguing one. No other sport has produced as many theories, locker-room stories, and jokes. Almost everyone has an opinion regarding the golf swing. There are advocates of the classical style, the ultra modern swing, and almost anything in between.

But what do we really know about the golf swing? This much: It is composed of several moving parts of the body, and of a long extension of the arm. It is designed to propel a small spherical object with varying configurations of dimples toward a 4½-inch hole in the ground. But beyond that, you may think that there are few other common elements.

Not so! We now know that there are parts of the golf swing that are governed by basic laws of physics that cannot change. These laws must be followed by every golfer in order to execute an effective swing. There are also principles of the golf swing that are directly related to the laws but are subject to each individual's judgment — as long as they do not violate or work against the laws. And, finally, there are preferences that allow each golfer to control his or her individual swing.

Keys to Effective Golf:
- Laws
- Principles
- Preferences

Most golfers want to understand their own swings so that they can correct them and continue to improve. This single factor — the search for the perfect swing — motivates most of us to continue practicing and ask questions about the swing itself. Fortunately, we now have some answers about the swing, and we know that there is no one perfect swing. In fact, many perfect swings are possible, so long as each obeys the laws of physics as they pertain to golf.

The search for the perfect swing has haunted sportsmen and women for centuries. There are literally hundreds of books written about the art of acquiring a good golf swing. Fortunately, one ardent golfer, Sir Ainsley Bridgland of London, pursued his quest for knowledge of the golf swing through scientific processes. He formed a research team consisting of professionals with training in biomechanics, engineering, anatomy, physical education, medicine, ergonomics and ballistics. These individuals discussed, dissected, analyzed, experimented with, and wrote about the golf swing. Their work resulted in a publication by physicist Alistair Cochran and golf writer John Stobbs, fittingly entitled: *The Search for The Perfect Swing* (Lippincott, 1968).

The conclusion from the years of work was a simple one — there is no perfect swing! Rather, there are many possible combinations of techniques which are both functional and correct. The only "perfect rule" is that in order to be an effective swing, each part of the swing must take advantage of the basic concepts of physics.

The final concluson of this research may have been a disappointment to Sir Ainsley Bridgland, but it is certainly a relief to golfers and golf instructors. Both the classical swing and the ultra modern swing are "right" if they are executed properly. Each swing can produce maximum results if it obeys the laws of physics, and is matched to the individual characteristics of the golfer and the golfer's equipment.

Your right to individualize the golf swing allows a great deal of flexibility. It does not, however, give you the right to violate the laws of physics. For example, if you hold the club with both palms facing the sky, it will be impossible to produce enough speed in the clubhead to send the ball very far. This grip may violate one of the laws of golf — speed.

Perhaps the best examples of individual swings can be seen among the outstanding golfers of the world. Spend one weekend watching a golf tournament, and you will discover many different styles of striking the ball. Each of the outstanding men and women have their own special preferences demonstrated in their swings. The only statement that can be made about their swings is that they are all different!

LAWS, PRINCIPLES, AND PREFERENCES

If there is no one perfect swing, can there be any understanding of the golf game? Yes! There are many effective ways to strike the golf ball.

Each of these effective techniques follows basic laws of golf (actually laws of physics as they pertain to golf).

Dr. Gary Wiren has proposed a model that explains the laws, principles, and preferences of golf. This model (called the LPP Model) explains the basic principles of physics that apply to golf, and the flexibility for applying these principles, which are available to each golfer. If you understand this model, you can become your own teacher. Each individual has a right to his or her own preferences as long as they do not contradict one another. Also, these preferences must match the principles that influence the application of the laws of the swing.

The laws, principles and preferences described by Wiren in his article "The Search for the Perfect Teaching Method" (*Professional Golfer*, April 1976) suggested a set of priorities for the golf swing. The first priority is the *laws*. These are invariable and happen no matter where or how the club contacts the ball. They include the relationship of speed, path, face, squareness of contact, and angle of approach to the flight of the ball. If you do not apply these laws properly, there is nothing you can do to change the result.

The *principles* of the swing are a second-level priority. They are limited in number and are specifically related to the laws of the golf swing. These are the mechanical aspects of the swing technique. They are generally discussed in terms of pre-swing or in-swing principles.

Preferences, the third level of priorities in the golf swing, are the choices you make as you combine the laws and principles. How close you stand to the ball when you swing, the type of grip you use, your stance, etc., can all have an impact on the swing, but there is no right or wrong as long as you effectively employ the laws and principles.

BALL FLIGHT LAWS

An understanding of the laws that affect the flight of the golf ball will answer many questions. If you understand the five ball flight laws, you will be able to figure out why you always slice, or why your ball always lands 20 yards short of Casey's.

Five Ball Flight Laws:
- Clubhead Speed
- Clubhead Path
- Clubhead Face
- Angle of Approach
- Squareness of Contact

Clubhead Speed

There is no substitute for swinging the club fast. Anyone who says you don't need to swing fast to hit the ball is trying to out-drive you. All other things being equal, a faster swung clubhead will always make the ball go farther.

Obviously, there may be trade-offs in accuracy and control if you try to swing the club too fast. But, once you have learned to control your body and the timing of your swing, the faster the club is traveling, the farther the ball will go. In fact, research has found that once you have reached about 65% of your maximum speed, the accuracy of the swing will actually increase.

Clubhead Path

If you plot the line along which the clubhead swings, you will be able to determine the initial direction in which the ball will travel. The path of the clubhead during the swing is the major factor determining the direction of the ball path. Some balls may curve off to one side or the other (due to "face" errors), but the direction of the ball flight will be primarily due to the path of the clubhead.

If your golf ball appears to be traveling straight but to the right or left of target, it is probably because of a "path error." Imagine playing baseball and being a right-handed batter trying to hit the ball to right field. You merely make your swing from inside to out, and stretch out toward right field as you make contact with the ball. The same thing happens in golf. If you consistently hit the ball on a straight line to the right of target, you are probably swinging with a path that points in that direction (Figure 2.1).

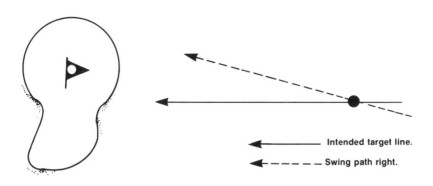

Intended target line.

Swing path right.

Figure 2.1. The diagram illustrates a swing path to the right of the intended target.

The reverse may be true if you consistently pull the ball. If your path is from outside in, you will move your clubhead on a line that points in the direction of the path of the ball. Checking your alignment and the path of your clubhead will usually correct these directional errors.

Clubhead Face

The alignment of the clubhead face relative to the path of the swing is the second factor that determines the direction of the ball. The face of the club can be square to the path, or it can be open or closed (Figure 2.2).

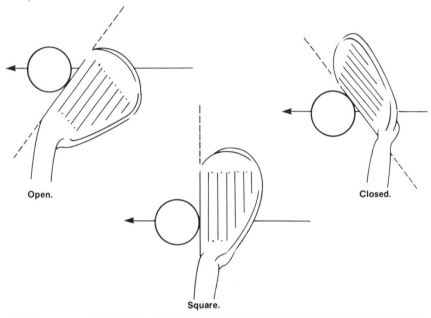

Figure 2.2. Blade alignment preferences.

The degree to which the clubface is open or closed at impact determines the amount of side spin imparted to the ball. This spin causes the path of the ball to curve while it is the air.

Watch the flight of your ball after you hit it. If your ball travels perfectly straight, both your clubhead path and clubhead face are square. If your ball travels off to one side of your target, you must ask yourself two questions:

- Did the ball travel straight, but to the right or left of target?
- Did the ball curve while in the air?

If the face of the club is open at impact, a sideward spin from left to right is produced (for right-handed golfers). If the face is closed at

13

impact, a sideward spin from right to left is produced. The more open or closed the clubface, the greater will be the spin imparted, and consequently the greater the curvature during the ball's flight. For example, a slightly open clubface produces a fade, whereas a slightly closed clubface produces a draw. As the face angle increases, the degree of curvature increases, with open clubfaces producing slices and closed clubfaces producing hooks.

If your ball flight tends to curve in either direction more than you like, your problem may be from one or two possible causes. First, check your alignment. If you are aligned properly, the cause may be your grip position, or hand action; an ineffective grip position or grip pressure may result in too much curvature in the flight of the ball.

Angle of Approach

The angle of the golf club as it approaches the ball will determine the height of the ball flight (Figure 2.3). Obviously, each golf club is designed to make the ball travel higher or lower, resulting in shorter or longer distances respectively. As the irons get higher in number (1-9) they will send the ball higher into the air because of the angle of the face. But within each club is a range of trajectories that are controlled by the angle of the golf club as it makes contact with the ball.

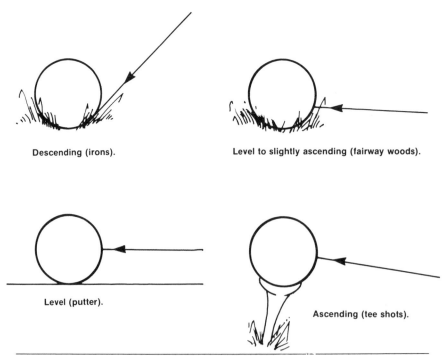

Descending (irons).

Level to slightly ascending (fairway woods).

Level (putter).

Ascending (tee shots).

Figure 2.3. The angle of approach determines the height of the ball flight.

A ball that is struck above its centerline will travel at a low angle. A ball that is struck below its center, or equator, will fly higher. In most cases it is to your advantage to strike the ball closer to the ground so that it will travel higher. One of the best ways to think about hitting a ball is to imagine the equator of the earth. Each time you strike the ball, think about hitting below the equator, in South America or Australia.

Squareness of Contact

A golf club is designed to be struck near the center of its face. Just as a tennis racket has a "sweet spot," a golf club has a special point, called the "centroid," that will produce maximum results in distance and direction control (Figure 2.4).

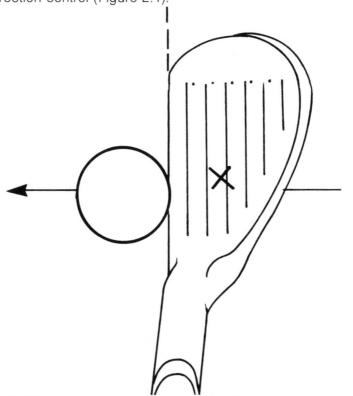

Figure 2.4. The centroid is the club's "sweet spot."

If you strike the ball with the club near the centroid, the ball will fly in a truer path, with better control. The more the contact point moves toward the heel or toe of the club, the more distance and control will deviate. Unfortunately, research shows that even the best golfers have trouble controlling this fine point on the head of the golf club.

15

Understanding the Laws

The ball flight laws explain many of the errors common to the game of golf. If you can apply these laws to your swing, you will be able to diagnose and correct many of the problems of your swing. For example:

- Too short or too long a ball flight is the result of inconsistent clubhead speed or angle of approach by the clubhead.
- Pushing or pulling the ball off to the right or left of the target is the result of the clubhead path.
- A hook or slice is the result of an incorrect clubhead face position at the moment of contact with the ball.
- A ball that is topped and does not leave the ground (worm burner!) or one that goes sky high, is the result of an incorrect angle of clubhead approach to the ball.
- A ball that reacts sharply off to the right or left is probably shanked or toed as a result of not contacting the ball squarely on the "sweet spot" of the club.

PRINCIPLES

In order to strike a golf ball that will travel straight toward the target, with maximum speed and square contact, you must follow the principles of the swing. These principles dictate the application of the laws to the golf ball. The swing principles can be considered in terms of both "pre-swing" and "in-swing" concepts.

The pre-swing principles allow you to get your body and the club into a position that can produce an efficient golf swing. There are three major pre-swing principles: grip, aim, and setup. The setup includes alignment, posture, weight distribution, ball position, and muscular tension.

Your grip on the club and your general relationship to the target largely determine your ability to apply the laws. If you are not in an efficient position, you will not be able to produce adequate speed or to deliver the club at the desired location.

The in-swing principles relate to the execution of the swing. There are nine in-swing principles: plane, width of arc, length of arc, lever system, timing, release, dynamic balance, swing center, and position of the target-side wrist and hand relative to the clubface position.

Pre-Swing Principles:
- Grip
- Aim
- Setup

In-Swing Principles:
- Plane
- Width of Arc
- Length of Arc
- Target-Side Hand and Wrist
- Lever System
- Timing

Release
- Dynamic Balance
- Swing Center

PRE-SWING PRINCIPLES

Grip

How you grip your club determines how you interact with the ball. The club controls the ball, and your hands control the club. Your hands are the only part of your body that come in contact with the golf club. Therefore your relationship with the club is determined by the way you hold it.

There are several variations of grips, although two positions are generally preferred: interlocking or overlapping (Figure 3.2). Both grips can be efficient, especially when you choose the one most suited and comfortable for you and your swing.

The grip has the greatest effect on the position of the clubface. Rotating your hands as little as one quarter inch can cause the face to open enough for a 40-yard slice! Much more emphasis should be placed on this one factor — check your grip each time you swing a club.

Aim

The alignment of your body and clubface as you begin to swing at the ball is tremendously important to the resultant ball flight. When you are standing at address in a neutral or square position, the clubface is aligned square to the target; that is, the face of the club is perpendicular to the line between the ball and the target. The body (feet, hips, and shoulders) is aligned parallel to the intended target line (Figure 3.6). This allows for the club to swing on the intended path for a longer period of time.

In this square position, the body can enhance the arm swing rather than restrict its motion in either direction. Alternatives to a square clubface (preferences toward open or closed) influence the path of the club, and, consequently, the path of the ball flight after impact.

17

Setup

Your setup can influence all five of the laws of the golf swing. The setup itself is a "ready position" that should allow the body to easily swing the golf club. It includes your posture, stance, weight distribution, muscular tension, and the placement of the ball relative to your body. The more consistent the setup, the more consistent the swing will become.

Your specific posture at address affects your swing motion. Individual postures may vary depending upon the amount of bend in the body at the address position (Figure 2.5). The extreme positions of excessive bend and lack of bend, or standing too tall, can reduce the effectiveness of the swing motion. A more neutral position is often preferred in order to enhance arm motion and body support in the swing.

The position of your ball at address affects the angle of approach and the resulting trajectory of the shot. How the ball is positioned in relation to the swing center is also an important aspect of the setup. A

Too far.   Too close.

Figure 2.5. Variations in posture affect the swing motion.

ball played forward in the stance will reduce the angle of approach if the swing center remains behind the ball at contact. This results in a higher shot. An example of this position is the driver setup. In contrast, a ball that is played farther back (away from the target) will result in a lower trajectory if the swing center is in front of the ball at impact. An example of this position is the one for the chip shot.

Weight distribution at address is yet another important aspect of setup. It allows for in-swing ease of motion. Distribution may vary from having your weight on your heel to having most of your weight on your toes. You can check your own preference for weight distribution by taking a normal stance over the ball. If you can lift your toes easily off the ground, you have your weight back on your heels. If you can lift your heels off the ground, you probably have a good, forward weight distribution.

IN-SWING PRINCIPLES

Plane of Swing

The plane of your swing is very important in golf. Your ideal plane is determined by your posture at address. The plane of swing is an imaginary inclined plane that extends from a point between your shoulders and ears, through the ball. A golfer who stands far away from the ball will have a rather flat plane, whereas someone who prefers to stand closer to the ball and more upright will have an upright plane. The level of plane can thus vary from flat to neutral to upright.

Width of Arc

There are two aspects of the arc of the swing: width and length. Both of these factors primarily affect the distance of potential flight of the ball.

The width of the arc refers to the radius of the swing. Assume that your target-side arm is the radius of a circle (the left arm for right-handed golfers). The longer that radius, the more potential speed the clubhead can develop. Therefore, theoretically, the more extended your arm, the more clubhead speed you develop. If you bend your arm, the width (radius) of the arc shortens, and therefore reduces the speed of the clubhead.

This principle suggests that your target-side arm should be straight in order to produce a maximum speed. However, many individuals are unable to fully extend their arms. Therefore a straight target arm may not be possible, though the closest approximation would probably be optimal.

19

Length of Arc

The length of your backswing determines how much speed can be developed in the downswing. On a short putt, you take a short backswing. For a longer shot you take a longer backswing, so that the forward swing has more time and space to develop speed.

The length of the backswing determines how much speed can be developed in the downswing. On a short putt, you take a short backswing. For a longer shot you take a longer backswing, so that the forward swing has more time and space to develop speed.

The length of the backswing (length of the arc) significantly determines the amount of speed that can be developed. This speed transfers directly to the force imparted on the ball, and subsequently to the distance that the ball travels. Therefore, the longer the backswing (circumference of the circle), the greater the speed, and therefore the force, that can be developed. Imagine yourself as a clock. The longer the hands are on your clock, the greater the length of the arc will be and therefore you will have more potential speed.

Target-Side Hand Position

The relationship of your target-side hand and the target-side arm at the top of the swing are very important. For right-handed golfers, this refers to the relationship between the left hand, left arm, and the club. By simply changing the position of your left hand, you can dramatically affect the position of the clubface at the top of the swing. Three positions are illustrated in Figure 2.6—cupped, square, and flexed. Take your normal grip position on the club and cock your wrist up, bringing the club pointing to the sky. This represents the position at the top of your swing and is determined by your grip position at address.

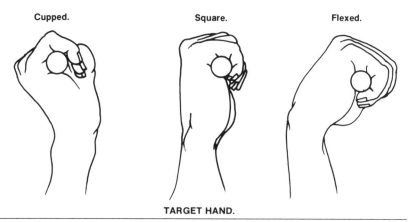

Cupped.　　Square.　　Flexed.

TARGET HAND.

Figure 2.6. The position of the target hand at the top of the swing is determined by the grip position at address.

Levers

Your target-side arm and the golf club act as one long arm. If you are right-handed, your left arm becomes part of the total lever. If your arm and club act as one unit, without bending, you are using a one-lever system. If you allow your wrist to cock in plane with your forearm, you have a two-lever system (Figure 2.7). Adding this second lever increases the force. That is, if you swing your arms and hands as one long club, you have only one lever and will hit the ball a shorter distance. Adding a wrist cock increases your distance because you now have two levers which, added together, produce more speed and force. This wrist cock will double the number of levers and approximately double your potential force.

Figure 2.7. The wrist cock produces a two-lever system.

Timing

The sequence of movements in the golf swing must be carefully timed to allow for efficiency and ease of motion. The timing of a golf swing is like the timing of a baseball batter. The timing is noted most often by which part moves first when initiating the backswing action: the hands, arms, shoulders, or legs. It is usually agreed that the last part moved on the backswing should initiate the forward swing, with all other parts moving in the reverse order. The movement generally starts with the backswing and flows from the hands to the arms, to the shoulders, to the hips, to the legs and then returns in the reverse order.

The golf swing is like a spring coiling up, and then uncoiling. One way to practice this is to think of three parts. The backswing starts with (1) hands and arms, then (2) shoulders, then (3) hips and legs. Then the swing returns forward—first with the hips and legs (3), then the shoulders (2), and finally the arms and hands (1). Thus the sequence is 1-2-3; 3-2-1.

Release

The timing of the golf swing is based on the ability to allow the hands and arms to return to their original position at the moment of contact—that is, release. If you can return your hands and arms to their starting position, it will free the power created in the backswing. This natural return to the starting position will allow the clubface to attain its maximum speed, along with good alignment. Most of the problems in release come when you try to force the hands to come around, or when you force the clubhead to close.

Problems in the release of the hands are often associated with tension and anxiety. Most golfers start to slice the ball when things are not going well. This is understandable because the lack of release is related to too much tension.

Dynamic Balance

Your body must be able to maintain its posture and balance throughout the golf swing. If you are falling off balance, you will lose some of the potential force you have developed in the backswing. Hitting a golf ball is like hitting a baseball or tennis ball. It requires the body to transfer all of its forces to the ball. You must start with your weight balanced, move it away from the desired direction of the ball, and then transfer it forward through the ball. If you shift your weight away from the target and then leave it there, you will not be able to hit the ball as far. You must shift your weight back and then forward, through the hitting zone. If you do shift it back to the starting point or beyond, you will lose power, change the arc of the swing, and impact the angle of approach.

Checklist for Swing Evaluation

Pre-Swing Front View
- Target Hand
  ☐top
  ☐neutral
  ☐under
- Rear Hand
  ☐top
  ☐neutral
  ☐under
- Stance
  ☐narrower than shoulders
  ☐shoulder width
  ☐wider than shoulders

In-Swing Front View
- Width of Arc at Impact
  ☐extended
  ☐collapsed
- Length of Arc
  ☐below parallel
  ☐parallel
  ☐short of parallel
- Position at the Top
  ☐cupped
  ☐square
  ☐hyperextended
- Lever
  ☐1
  ☐2
  ☐3
- Release
  ☐early
  ☐tuned
  ☐late
  ☐no
- Dynamic Balance
  ☐yes, controlled
  ☐no, falls back
  ☐no, falls forward
  ☐no, stationary
- Posture
  ☐weight rear foot
  ☐weight even
  ☐weight target foot
- Backswing Timing
  ☐hand
  ☐arm
  ☐shoulder
  ☐leg

- Forward Swing Timing
  ☐hand
  ☐arm
  ☐shoulder
  ☐leg
- Address Swing Center
  ☐back of ball
  ☐even with ball
  ☐forward of ball
- Backswing Swing Center
  ☐back of ball
  ☐even with ball
  ☐forward of ball
- Forward Swing Swing Center
  ☐back of ball
  ☐even with ball
  ☐forward of ball

Pre-Swing Down the Line View
- Blade Alignment
  ☐open
  ☐square
  ☐closed
- Feet Alignment
  ☐open
  ☐square
  ☐closed
- Hip Alignment
  ☐open
  ☐square
  ☐closed
- Shoulder Alignment
  ☐open
  ☐square
  ☐closed
- Heel-Toe Weight Distribution
  ☐weight on heels
  ☐weight even
  ☐weight forward
- Body Inclination at Address
  ☐sitting back
  ☐over ball
  ☐standing tall

In-Swing Down the Line View
- Plane
  ☐upright
  ☐in plane
  ☐flat

23

Swing Center

Imagine your golf swing as a ferris wheel. There is a center to that wheel that lies somewhere under your chin, near the center of your sternum. This center is the point around which the arc of your swing is made. It is important for this center to return to its starting position as you make contact with the ball.

The swing center is sometimes related to the position of your head. As your head shifts backward, the swing center may also shift. This is not necessarily bad, as long as it returns to its starting position when you hit the ball. Most good golfers shift their swing centers slightly away from the ball and then return through the ball at contact. The trick is to get it back over the ball at contact. If you don't you alter the arc of the swing and violate the laws related to angle of approach and speed. Your golf swing is merely an expression of your application of these laws and principles. Once you understand the laws and principles, you will be able to diagnose your problems and work toward correcting them.

PREFERENCES

Preferences related to individual choices about what "feels right" for you. There are countless potential preferences, but not all will be compatible with your application of the laws and principles. Just make sure that the preferences you choose do not sacrifice the application of the laws.

For example, you may wish to use a grip that shows three knuckles on top, versus one that has two knuckles showing. That is fine as long as you can still keep the club in the desired plane, contact the ball squarely, develop adequate speed, etc.

Your preference should reflect your style of play, and perhaps your personality. You must choose what type of grip: three-knuckle, two-knuckle, or one-knuckle. You must also choose a swing tempo: slow, medium, or fast. You must also choose a stance and alignment: open, closed, or square. And on and on. There are many different preferences from which to choose. Just be sure to make your preferences complementary so that you can use the laws and principles to your best advantage.

It is always important to check the compatibility of the laws and principles within your swing. The following checklist was designed to help you systematically analyze each component.

3

BASIC SWING TECHNIQUES

All golfers have certain things in common. They have an idea of where they want the ball to go. They hold the club. They position their body in order to swing. They swing the club back away from the ball in order to swing forward at the ball. Their objective is to contact the ball.

From the last chapter you learned that regardless of your stage of golf development, from the beginner to the elite player, the basic fundamentals of the swing are common to all players. The difference is found in the efficiency and refinement of the swing motion and the ability to modify the principles to influence the laws.

Through the laws, principles, and preferences, all of us have an opportunity to understand the golf swing better. The mystique that has surrounded the game since its inception is slowly being removed. This chapter and the one to follow is based on the Laws, Principles, and Preferences Model (LPP). The intent of this chapter is to provide you with a better conceptual understanding of the golf swing, that is, full swing and short game.

FULL SWING

When you first view the golf swing, it may seem quite complex, with many moving parts. Let's reduce its complexity by describing the swing with adjectives of motion: rhythmic, flowing, continuous, repeatable, pendular. Now let's describe the swing with word pictures that depict the motion adjectives: a swing in the park, a ferris wheel with a tilt, a wheel, a pendulum. When viewed as a total motion, the parts begin to blend, each contributing its share.

With a holistic view of motion in mind, the principles of the LPP Model will be presented with preferences for technique application. For many of you this may be new, for others a review. Whatever your level of skill, good fundamentals are essential.

25

PRE-SWING FUNDAMENTALS

Grip

The grip is the most important fundamental. Your hands are the only communication link you have with the club. It is recommended that your hands be positioned on the club with the palms facing each other (Figure 3.1). This allows the hands to work as a unit during the swing.

Target Hand

- Hold the club by your target side with the face of the club pointed toward an imaginary target.
- With your arm and hand relaxed, grip the club as if you were shaking hands with the club.
- Raise the club from the ground. The head of the club will be pointing forward at approximately chest height.

Figure 3.1. Placing the target and rear hands on the club the same way each time is important.

Rear Hand

Maintaining the above position, extend your rear hand as if to shake hands with the club.

The relationship between your rear-side and target-side hands should provide a comfortable link between you and your club. There are two primary connecting positions designed to provide unity to the grip: the overlapping and interlocking grips (Figure 3.2).

Overlap

Place the little finger of the rear hand between the index and middle finger of the target hand.

Interlock

Join the little finger of the rear hand with the index finger of the target hand.

26

Overlap.

Interlock.

Figure 3.2. The relationship between the two hands.

These two grip positions provide the fundamental link between the club and the body. In order to insure good club control, you may wish to examine the three checkpoints listed:

- Imaginary V's formed by the index finger and thumb of both hands point to the rear side (non-target side) of your chin.
- The club is held diagonally across the palm in the target hand, forming a palm and finger grip. The fingers of the rear hand, rather than the palm, hold the club (Figure 3.3).
- Two knuckles are visible on the target and rear hands (Figure 3.4).

27

Diagonally across the palm of the target hand.   Fingers of the rear hand.

Figure 3.3. Checkpoints for the grip.

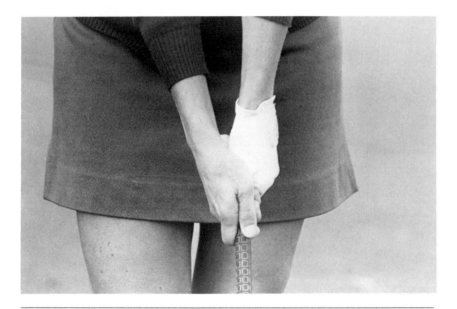

Figure 3.4. The neutral grip position.

This is a neutral grip position. Depending upon your individual needs, the grip position may be modified; however, you should maintain the palms-facing position (that is, hands in praying fashion). To increase hand action, the hands may be moved slightly to the rear side. To decrease hand action, the hands move slightly to the target side (Figure 3.5).

28

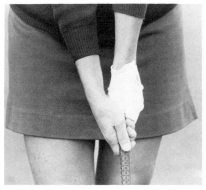 

| Shift to rear side. | Shift to target side. |

Figure 3.5. Grip alternatives for increasing (shift to rear side) and decreasing (shift to target side hand action).

Setup

The setup provides the basis of movement. Think about the position a shortstop takes prior to a pitch, or the position of a guard on a football or basketball team, or of a parent receiving an on-rushing child. These are basic ready positions that prepare and allow free and efficient movement when needed.

Your golf setup provides you with that same "ready" feeling. You should strive to be consistent to the point of being methodical in taking your setup. This will produce a more consistent swing. Additionally, as will be discussed later, your setup routine will be a means of mental preparation.

Alignment

Next to your grip, alignment is most important for developing a consistent and efficient swing. Imagine a marksman shooting a rifle with a curved barrel. What are his chances of hitting the target? Very low! Swinging the golf club without precise alignment ranks with shooting with a curved barrel.

Consider the golf swing as a motion back from and through to a target. The more consistent your alignment toward the target, the more repeatable the motion becomes. Imagine a railroad track, or two parallel lines. The ball is on one line (i.e., target line), which extends to your target. Your feet are on the other line (i.e., body line), which, when extended, will be parallel to the target line. It is suggested that your feet, hips, and shoulders be parallel to the direction you wish the ball to go (Figure 3.6). This parallel alignment is known as a square stance.

29

Square stance.

Open stance.

Closed stance.

Figure 3.6. Stance variations.

Individual needs may require a more closed or a more open stance (Figure 3.6). The closed stance tends to increase the body turn away from the target while restricting the forward motion toward the target. The open stance tends to be more restricting on the backswing and freer on the forward swing toward the target.

30

Width of Stance

The stance width allows you to be balanced and mobile during the swing motion. A stance with the feet about shoulder-width apart (measured from the inside of the heels) provides a good base for motion. A stance that is too wide restricts motion, and one that is too narrow tends to inhibit motion. If you are relatively tall, you may want to try a slightly wider stance. If you are quite short, you may want to try a narrower stance.

Posture

Posture is important for efficiency of motion, freedom from tension, and readiness to move. Consistent or efficient motion is hard to produce when the body is too close or too far from the ball at address, when it is too upright or slumped, or when there is excessive tension.

The following guidelines will provide you with efficient posture:
- Stand erect with your back straight and weight distributed evenly between your feet.
- Bend forward from the top of your thighs, keeping your body straight at about a 45^0 angle. Note: A club may be used, as illustrated in Figure 3.7 to help obtain the position. Keep the club in contact with your back as you bend. In Figure 3.7, the club moves off the back. This is not desired.
- Your arms and hands should be relaxed and hanging freely from your shoulders.
- Bend your knees slightly while maintaining your position.
- The weight distribution will be more forward on your foot, from the midstep to the balls of your feet.

Ball Position

The ball is positioned at address at the lowest point of the full-swing arc. If the golf swing were a perfect pendular motion and only the arms were involved in the swing, the ball would be positioned in the center of the stance. However, in the golf swing, the lower body action moves the lowest point of the arc closer to the target side of center for the irons, and toward the target heel with the woods. Note: With specialty shots the ball position varies with desired trajectory.

You can determine your ball position by taking practice swings, noting where you consistently contact the ground. This may vary as your swing techniques improve. The more active your leg drive becomes and the later your release is maintained, the more the ball is positioned toward the target side. Ball position for the woods and irons is illustrated in Figure 3.8.

Figure 3.7. Obtaining the desired posture by using a club.

Figure 3.8. Ball position for the woods and irons.

FULL SWING MOTION

Now that you have established your pre-swing fundamentals, you are ready to put them into action. The stages of the golf swing are presented sequentially in the following illustrations and are used with permission of the National Golf Foundation (1981) (Figure 3.9). Front view and rear view are presented. Together, they will enable you to put the basic fundamentals of the swing into better perspective.

Address:
- Feet shoulder-width apart.
- Club an extension of target arm.
- Ball forward of center in stance.
- Body in "ready" position.
- Weight set inside rear knee and foot.

Figure 3.9. Stages of the golf swing—full swing sequence.

Takeaway Sequence:
- Hands-arms-shoulders.
- Hub steady and behind ball.

Half-Swing Backswing:
- Target arm extends, rear arm hinges.
- Wrist cock by hip height.
- Weight begins to shift to rear side.

Figure 3.9. Continued

34

Top of the Swing:
- Back to the target.
- Weight shifted to inside of rear foot.
- Hub remains steady.

Half-Swing, Forward Swing:
- Legs drive laterally toward target.
- Arms follow.
- Hands delay.

Figure 3.9. Continued

Impact:
- Weight shifted to target side.
- Hands and arms produce "square" clubface at impact.
- Hub remains steady behind the ball.
- Clubhead at maximum speed.

Through Impact:
- Arms rotate after impact.
- Hub remains steady.

Figure 3.9. Continued

36

Finish:
* **Arms and hands in high finish.**
* **Majority of weight on target foot.**
* **Body faces target.**

Figure 3.9. Continued

No doubt you are wondering how anyone can think of so much. They can't! Once you understand how the parts contribute to the total motion of the swing, you will begin to "chunk" the parts into larger wholes. Word keys often aid in this process. The keys are usually helpful when they are in pairs relating a motion back from and through to a target. Some examples of word keys are "coiling and uncoiling," "stretch and spring," "load and unload," "load and fire," "turn back and turn through." There is no magic in these keys. You may want to try these or you may want to use others. Whichever keys you decide to use, it is important that you experiment to find what works best for you.

FULL SWING PRACTICE SUGGESTIONS

The practice ideas that follow will help you begin to put your swing into motion. The first three objectives use mimetic drills. These will help you feel the motion of the swing without actually swinging a club. These drills can be done at home, inside or outside, or as a warmup to practice or play. They help you "feel" rather than "think" about your swing. Objective 4 allows you to build upon your swing motion using a club. As you work through the objectives, continue to refer to the full-swing sequence illustrated in Figure 3.9. Try to visualize the motions as you do them.

You should begin your full-swing practice with a 5-, 6-, or 7-iron. The motion you develop through these objectives and drills will be used for all clubs. The change in club length as the club number decreases or increases is easy to adapt to in your setup position. Begin with the irons, then once your swing is more grooved, advance to the woods. Ball position will move from the target side of center with your irons to the inside of target side with your woods. The setup position remains the same for both irons and woods.

Objective 1
To develop a feel for the setup position.

Drills
1. Stand with your feet about shoulder-width apart. Take your posture position as was illustrated in Figure 3.7, using a club.
   Note: Put the club on the ground after you take your position.
   • Do you feel your arms hanging freely from your shoulders?
   • Do you feel your weight from midstep to the balls of your feet? Without changing your position, is it easier to tap your heels or tap your toes?

2. Take your setup position. To feel the undesired position, sit back as if to sit on a stool.
   • Do your arms feel as relaxed as when you are bending over more?
   • Is it easier to tap your heels or your toes?
   (Note: You should feel more restricted sitting back.)

3. Take your desired setup. Try to feel the difference between being over the ball and relaxed in your arms and sitting back and being restricted.
   • Stand with your heels on a 2" X 4" and take your desired setup.
   • What do you feel?
   • Stand with toes on a 2" X 4" (Figure 3.10) and take your desired setup. What do you feel?
   • Which of the two positions provides the greater mobility?

Figure 3.10. The boards help establish a feel for the heel-toe weight distribution at address.

Objective 2

To feel the motion of the swing.

Drills

1. Take your setup position. Let your arms hang freely, with the palms of your hands facing each other but not touching (Figure 3.11). Stand, swinging your arms back and forth in a pendular motion. Your arms should feel light and relaxed.

- Gradually let your lower body take on the rhythm of your arms—target knee touches your rear knee, touches your target knee. You continue to swing higher. Note: Allow your target heel to come off the ground slightly.
- Do you feel the weight shifting from one side to the other?
- Do your arms feel light and swinging?

39

Figure 3.11. Mimetic drills enhance motion awareness in the early stages of learning.

Word Keys:
- Back to target-belt buckle to target
- Back-through
- Coil-uncoil
- Turn back-turn through
- Motion away-motion to

Objective 3

To feel the swinging motion about a fixed center.

The following visualizations may help you conceptualize the swing turn:
- Visualize your head as the hub of a wheel and your arms as the spokes.
- Take your setup position and imagine a rod running down your back. Swing around the rod.

Drill

With a partner, repeat the drills in Objective 2. Have your partner place a hand on your head as a reminder not a hold. Make the swinging motion, feeling the turn.
- Do you feel a difference in your posture on both the backward and forward swing?
- Do you feel stretching in the upper part of your back on the target side?

Figure 3.12. The Whoosher Drill provides the feeling of target-side awareness.

Objective 4

To feel the swing motion while swinging a club.

Drills

1. Wide Whoosher Drill—Hold the club in your target hand just above the hosel. Turn the club in front of you, parallel to the ground and with the grip end pointing away from an imaginary target. Grip the club with the fingers of your rear hand, palm up. Your hands should be shoulder-width apart (Figure 3.12).

Set your setup position. Let your arms hang freely, holding the club in the above manner. Make your full swing motion to the top of the backswing. Let go with your rear hand and pull down with your target arm. The club should make a swishing sound. Note: Your lower body responds—target knee to rear knee, rear knee to target knee.

- Do you hear a swishing sound? If not, make sure your body is moving.

2. Repeat the Whoosher Drill. Have a partner extend a club, holding it at the hosel. Place the grip end on your head as a "reminder." Note: The club is an extension of the partner's arm—partner is now farther away.

- Do you hear the swishing sound?
- Do you feel a difference in your posture with the "reminder?"
- Do you feel your lower body motion?

41

Note: If your posture is not maintained as you swing, or if you move up and down, the swing motion is reduced and becomes ineffective.

3. Repeat the Whoosher Drill without a partner.

4. Taking your setup position prior to swinging, grip the club in the normal manner. (Refer to the procedure previously described.) Stand erect with your feet together. Extend your arms in front of your body. Bend from the top of your thighs. Maintain the extension of your arm and club until the club touches the ground. Move your feet shoulder-width apart. This is your setup position.

Maintain your setup position. Open your hands and let the club drop.
- Do your arms hang freely in the same position? Do they relax and come in toward your body? Or do they relax and move away from your body?
Note: Your arms should be relaxed and remain in the same position when you drop the club. If your arms come in, you are too far away.

5. Repeat Exercise 4 until you feel comfortable taking your setup position.

6. Take your setup position with the club. Repeat the same motion you used when swinging without the club (Objective 2).
- Let the club brush the ground back and through.
- Keep the motion continuous, flowing from one side to the other. Let your arms swing higher and higher.
- Allow your lower body to feel the rhythm.

7. Repeat Exercise 6 with a partner holding a club on your head.

Checkpoints:

Backswing
- Back to target
- Target knee touching rear knee
- Hands to the sky

Forward Swing
- Belt Buckle to the target
- Rear knee touching target knee
- Hands to the sky

Swing Motion
- Rear-side motion looks like target-side motion
- Mirror images on rear and target sides

8. Pick out a spot—a piece of grass, a tee, anything but a ball. Take your setup position relative to that spot. Make full swings, swinging through that spot.
- Do you feel the swing motion, back and through?

9. Place a ball on the tee, one half inch above the ground. Make your full swings. Allow the ball to get in the way of your swing.
- Back—through—hold.
- Review your checkpoints—belt buckle to target, hands to the sky, and rear knee into target knee.
- Repeat the drill.

Keep hitting off the tee until consistent contact is made. Gradually lower the tee until it is at ground level.

Drills help you feel the motion of your swing. As you began, the motion may have seemed different or awkward, probably because of the focus on posture. The lower-body motion allows you to maintain your posture more easily. This should have been clearly felt during these drills.

Practice the drills with a partner (Figure 3.13). This will help you see the motion you want to achieve as well as gain a better understanding of why the drills can enhance your learning.

Figure 3.13. Partner drills are fun.

SHORT GAME

The short game is broken down into mini-swings, putting, and sand shots. This phase of the game emphasizes greater accuracy with the distance component. Because strength is not a factor in the short game, you can become extremely proficient very quickly. As your long game improves, the short game helps prompt lower scores.

Mini-Swings

Mini-swings are smaller portions of the full swing. Once you reach the point where your full swing with a 9-iron sends the ball over the green, you need to begin using mini-swings. The mini-swings presented here are the one-lever and two-lever swings. The one-lever swing is a pendular action with no wrist or hand action. The two-lever swing uses wrist-cock and hand action. The full swing is also a two-lever swing. The distance and trajectory you desire will determine which club and swing you choose. The mini-swings differ from the full swing in the distance desired, the length of the swing, and the setup position.

Let's consider the golf swing as symmetrical, that is, the length of the backswing equals the length of the forward swing. One way to conceptualize the symmetrical swing lengths is to think of a wheel, as illustrated in Figure 3.14. The numerical notations represent swing lengths illustrated by the arm and hand position. The lowest point represents the address position at the ball.

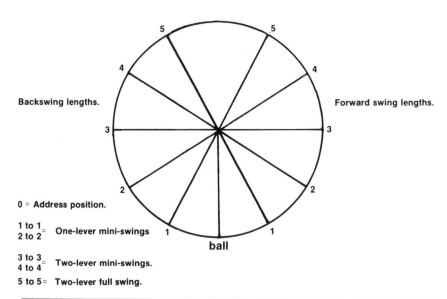

Figure 3.14. Wheel concept of swing lengths.

ONE-LEVER MINI-SWING

The one-lever swing is usually referred to as the chip shot. The purpose of this shot is to land the ball on the green safely and have it roll to the pin. The intent is to have a low trajectory for control. This shot is characterized as having more roll time than air time. The setup position for a one-lever swing is illustrated in Figure 3.15.

Setup.

Backswing.

Forward swing.

Figure 3.15. The one-lever mini-swing provides for simplicity.

45

One-Lever Position Checkpoints:

Stance
- Feet fairly close together
- Slightly open stance
- More weight on the target foot

Posture
- Knees flexed
- Arms hanging freely
- Choke down on the club.

Ball Position
- Rear side of center

Swing Center
- Arms and hands ahead of the ball

Club Position
- Delofted

The setup position is important because it allows you to achieve the desired result most efficiently. In this position the hands and arms work as a unit, back and through with little to no motion in the lower body. This minimizes the error potential.

In order to remove the loft from the club, position the ball slightly to the rear side of center of your stance. Your arms, hands, and swing center should be in front of the ball. The back ball position helps insure lower trajectory with more control and provides contact with the ball at the lowest point of the swing arc.

The one-lever technique can be used with any club. However, it is most effective with the 5 through 9 irons. When selecting the club, remember that the more green between the ball and pin, the less loft should be used. Similarly the less green between the ball and the pin, the more lofted a club you should use (Figure 3.16). The loft softens the shot by decreasing the roll.

The length and pace of the swing determine the distance. The longer the swing and the faster the swing pace, the greater the distance obtained. You will find through practice that the less lofted clubs have less air time and more roll time compared with the more lofted clubs. With the same swing and pace, the less lofted clubs will roll farther than the more lofted clubs.

Figure 3.16. Use more loft when there's less green to work with.

TWO-LEVER MINI-SWING

The two-lever mini-swing is illustrated by the 3-to-3 and 4-to-4 swing lengths. Once the arms reach hip height, the wrists have cocked in a half-swing position. This shot is usually referred to as a pitch shot. The intent of this shot is to produce a higher trajectory. It is characterized by having more air time with less ground time. The setup position is illustrated in Figure 3.17.

Setup.

Backswing.

Forward swing.

Figure 3.17. Two-lever mini-swing sequence.

Two-Lever Setup Position Checkpoints:

Stance
- Feet a little less than shoulder width
- Square to slightly open stance
- Weight evenly distributed between both feet

Posture
- Normal posture for full swing

Ball Position
- Center of stance

Swing Center
- Arms and hands even with the ball

Club Position
- Square

The setup position is similar to the regular full swing. The swing produces more of a sweeping action through the ball. This particular type of shot and setup requires a good lie. That is, the ball should be on the surface of the ground as opposed to in a divot or deep rough.

The swing motion will have a small amount of weight shift in the lower body to accommodate the longer swing. However, the shift will be less than that used in the full swing.

The two-lever mini-swing is most effective with the pitching wedge and sand wedge because of the higher desired trajectory. This shot is used for going over traps when approaching the green or shooting to tight pin placements where there is not enough green space for the ball to land and roll (Figure 3.18).

SHORT GAME PRACTICE SUGGESTIONS

Your short game can be practiced at home, in a park, or at a golf course. The short game strokes are quickly acquired because they require less motion. The objectives that follow place a heavy emphasis on the development of technique. Once you have the technique, it becomes easier to concentrate on the feel for distance.

The differences in your setup from the full swing to the mini-swings should be noted (Figure 3.19). Your setup position for the mini-swings allows you to execute the desired shots. Be meticulous in taking your setup each time. It will pay off by developing consistency. Table 3.1 is provided as a review and reference for the setup positions for the full swing, mini-swings, putting and sand shots. Refer to it often.

Figure 3.18. The two-lever mini-swing is used to obtain loft as, for example, when going over traps.

1-to-1 and 2-to-2.

3-to-3 and 4-to-4.

5-to-5.

Figure 3.19. Comparison of the setup positions for mini-swings and full swing.

Table 3.1
Guide for the Setup Positions
of the
Full Swing and Short Game Strokes

	Full Swing	One-Lever	Two-Lever	Putting	Sand
Grip	regular	regular and choked down on shaft	regular	palms up	regular
Stance	shoulder-width, alignment square	narrow, slightly open	narrow, square	shoulder-width, square	shoulder-width, slightly open
Ball Position	center to target heel	rear side of center	center	center to target side	target to rear side center
Clubface	square	square	square	square	square to open
Swing Length	5-to-5	1-to-1 or 2-to-2	3-to-3 or 4-to-4		3-to-3 to 5-to-5
Swing Center	rear side to even with the ball	target side of ball	even with the ball	rear side to even with	target side to even with the ball
Weight	even on both feet	target side	target side to even	even to target side (varies with ball position)	even to target side (varies with lie)

Objective 1

To become more aware of the differences in the setup position between the full swing and one-lever mini-swings.

Drills

1. Take your full swing setup with a ball. Now take your one-lever mini-swing setup position.
   - What is the difference in the stance (width and alignment)?
   - What is the difference in the weight distribution?
   - What is the difference in the position of the swing center?
   - What is the difference in the grip length?
   - What is the difference in the ball position?

2. Repeat, taking your full swing position and then your mini-swing position until you become comfortable going back and forth.

Objective 2

To feel the motion of the one-lever mini-swings.

Drills

1. Without a club, take your setup position. Let your arms hang freely. Place your hands together, palms facing ("praying" hands). Point your fingers to the rear side, maintaining extended arms. Move your arms back and forth in a pendular motion.
   - The motion you feel with your arms and shoulders will be similar with a club. In this position your hands are inactive and the arms and shoulders direct the motion — straight back and straight through, with the backswing equal to the forward-swing length.

2. Using a 7, 8, or 9 iron, place two clubs on the ground, parallel and just wider than the width of your club. Direct the clubs toward a target (Figure 3.20). Take your setup position, with your club between the parallel clubs and square to your target. Using your one-lever pendular motion, swing the club back and forth in the parallel clubs. Maintain the square blade position as you swing the club in the track. Alternate every five swings from a 1-to-1 to 2-2-2 swing length.
   Note Figure 3.15: The address position of the arms and club is maintained on the back and forward swings.
   Swing back, through, and then hold your follow-through to check that the position is the same.
   - Blade is square to the target.
   - The clubhead has not passed your hands.
   - Back of the target hand is facing the target.

53

Figure 3.20. Parallel clubs provide a feel for the path.

3. Using the parallel clubs as a path guide, hit balls toward a designated target, for example, 15 feet (Figure 3.20).
  - Check your finish position on each shot.
  - Remember — back, through, and hold.
  - Alternate 1-to-1 and 2-to-2 swing lengths every five shots, initially using a 7, 8, or 9 iron. Note the difference in distance in the swing lengths.
  - Alternate clubs and swing lengths (for example, a 7 iron for 1-to-1 and 2-to-2, etc.) note the difference in trajectory and distance.

54

Setup.

Backswing.

Forward swing.

Active hands.

Figure 3.21. An extended shaft is a good teaching aid.

4. Holding a second club as illustrated in Figure 3.21, make practice swings as described. If your hands become too active so that the clubhead passes your hands through impact, the shaft will hit your target side as illustrated in the active-hands sequence.

55

Figure 3.22. Clubs make good targets for distance practice.

Objective 3

To become aware of the motion requirements for various distances. Place targets at distances of 15, 25, 35, and 40 feet (Figure 3.22).

Drill

Using the one-lever mini-swings and the same club, hit five balls to each target. Begin with the 9-iron and work back to a 5-iron (no parallel clubs).

- What is the difference in air time using the same club as the length requirements vary?
- What is the difference in roll, using the same club, as the distance varies?
- What is the difference in air time and roll between the various clubs at the same distance? Various distances?

Objective 4

To become more aware of the differences in the setup position between the one-lever and two-lever mini-swings.

Drills

1. Take your one-lever setup with a ball. Now take your two-lever mini-swing setup position.
   - What is the difference in the stances (width and alignment)?
   - What is the difference in the position of the swing center?
   - What is the difference in the grip length?
   - What is the difference in the ball position?

2. Repeat until you feel comfortable going back and forth between the two.

Objective 5

To feel the motion of the two-lever mini-swings.Use a pitching wedge or sand wedge.

Drills

1. Practice swings, making a 3-to-3 swing length. Place a tee in the grip end of the club. The tee should point to the ground on the backswing (3) and on the forward swing (3).

2. Hit balls, with the tee in the grip end, toward a target 30 yards out (for example, 3-to-3).
   - Check the tee on the backswing and forward swing.
   - What is the difference in the swing feel from the 2-to-2 to the 3-to-3 swing?
   - What is the difference in trajectory?

3. Place targets at 30, 40, 50, and 70 yards. Hit five shots to each target.
   - What is the difference in swing feel for the various distances?

4. Practice swings, using the 4-to-4 swing length and 3-to-3 swing length.
   - What is the difference in swing feel?

5. Hit balls, using the 4-to-4 swing length toward a target set at 80 yards (or less for your swing level).

6. Alternate shots, using the 3-to-3 and 4-to-4 swing lengths. Direct your target shots within the distance comfortable for your swing control.

PUTTING

Putting is a very important phase of the game. A putt of six inches counts the same as a beautiful 250-yard drive. However, because putting is not as exciting as trying to hit the long drives, less attention is usually given to putting in practice. Yet, with an understanding of the technique and with practice, you can become an excellent putter.

The putting stroke is a ground stroke that rolls the ball. The intent is to strike the ball as squarely as possible on the path that the ball is to roll. To accomplish this, the putting stroke should be simple, with few moving parts.

Putting is very individual, from the type of grip used, to the stance, to the style of putter. The preferences in putting styles are easily observed among tour professionals, amateurs, and recreational golfers.

Good putters have four technique components in common: eyes directly over or slightly behind the ball; balance; square blade relative to intended path; and the blade on path, back, and through the ball. Their preferences for setup may vary, but their actual execution is similar.

Technique Review:
- Eyes over or slightly behind the ball
- Balance
- Square blade
- Square path

Figure 3.23. Variations in putting grips.

Because the putter design is more upright than the iron or wood design, a modification in the full-swing grip is necessary. The following putting grips (Figure 3.23) illustrate various combinations of hand placement as contrasted with the full-swing grip.

The grip you select should allow your hands to work as a unit. The less active your hands are in the stroke, the better. The hands tend to be more subject to slight changes in day-to-day pressures, which could affect the consistency and control of your stroke distance and direction.

The putting stroke, as the one-lever mini-swing, is best characterized as a pendular motion. The length of the backswing is equal to the length of the forward swing. The hands, arms, and shoulders work as a unit with no involvement of the lower body. The lower body provides the balance and support foundation. Because the putting stroke is short and precise, motion should be minimized without imposing tension.

59

The posture you select for putting will enhance your stroke efficiency. You should try to feel the same posture as for your full swing — your arms hang freely from your shoulders, there is a bend from the top of the thighs, and a slight flex in the knees. This posture helps reduce the tension in your shoulders and arms. You will be closer to the ball because the putter is shorter and more upright. The posture position will also allow you to have your eyes over the ball more, or slightly behind it on the putting line.

Your stance is a preference. However, your shoulders should be parallel to the target line. If you are just starting to play, you may want to begin with a square stance, with your shoulders, hips, and feet parallel to the target line. You should feel comfortable and balanced. A wide, narrow, pigeon-toed, or any other foot position is your choice.

Ball position in putting is determined by your weight distribution at address. This becomes a preference and is determined by your setup position. If your weight is evenly distributed, the ball position will tend to be on the target side of center. If your weight is set more toward the target side, the ball will be positioned closer to the target foot. It is recommended that the ball position not extend beyond the target foot. This tends to alter the shoulder alignment from parallel and could reduce the effectiveness of the stroke.

A variety of positions allow your arms, hands, and shoulders to work as a unit. Two of these are illustrated in Figure 3.24. Each of these positions allows for the eyes over the ball, balance, a square blade, and a square path.

Putters, as do irons and woods, have a center point (centroid). When contacted at this point, the most consistent results are produced for both direction and distance. This center point should be marked on the putter. The center point is found by holding the putter in the air with the index finger and thumb so that it is hanging freely. With the back of a pencil, your finger, or a golf ball, tap the blade lightly (Figure 3.25). The point at which the blade moves back with the least vibration or movement at either the toe or heel and produces a solid feel is the center point. All putters, with or without lines, should be checked. The lines put on by the manufacturers may not always be exact.

A stroke that strikes the ball off the putter's center point results in a greater deviation from the desired direction and distance. For example, a putt that contacts the ball closer to the heel or toe of the blade rather than at the center point produces a sideward spin that influences the direction. If the putt is struck on the desired target path but closer to the heel side of the center point, the ball will tend to spin away from the hole on that side. The results are the same for the toe side of the contact point.

Figure 3.24. Variations in putting postures.

Figure 3.25. Determine centroid of the putter by tapping with a ball.

Distance loss is also evident from an off-center hit in either the toe or heel direction. For example, assume the desired distance for a putt is 20 feet. If you contact two putts on the desired path with the desired swing pace for 20 feet, the on-center hit will go the desired distance, whereas the off-center hit will fall short of the desired distance.

Using the suggested pendular motion, the arm, hands, and shoulder unit established by your grip and posture may become quite consistent in direction and distance. The direction is preset by your blade alignment and body alignment parallel to the target line.

The distance factor in putting is gauged by a combination of the stroke length (i.e. equal length on the backward and forward swings), on-center hits, and the pace or speed of the stroke. Through practice, you will be able to determine the length and pace for different distances.

As you practice, try to develop a stroke that is compact and relatively short in order to develop greater consistency and control. A smooth stroke with a consistent swing pace is dependable. A stroke that is too long, too short, or jerky, for example, requires more control; too often, control is lost. The putts become erratic. They go either too fast or too short, and deviate from the desired direction.

PUTTING PRACTICE SESSIONS

No matter how well you strike the ball from tee to green, your putting ability will make the end difference in becoming a mediocre, average, or fine player. Developing a good putting technique will help you lower your scores.

Technique can be practiced at home more effectively than on a practice green. At home you can concentrate on the feel of the technique without immediate concern for the result. When practicing on a green, the technique can be good, but because of the irregularities in the greens, the results may provide inaccurate information. This may cause you to make unnecessary stroke adjustments to accommodate the greens.

The following practice suggestions encourage you to develop stroke technique at home (Objectives 1-4) and distance and feel awareness at the course or practice green (Objectives 5 and 6). When you play, your objective is to trust your technique so that you can concentrate on alignment and feel for distance.

Objective 1

To develop feel for the putting setup.

Drills

1. Take your putting setup to a ball as presented in Table 3.1.

Checkpoints:
- Eyes over or slightly behind the ball
- Feel balanced
- Square blade
- Square shoulders
- Arms hanging freely
- Blade flat on the ground

---

2. Have a partner check your setup position while looking down the target line.

Objective 2

To feel the pendular motion of the stroke without a ball.

Drill

Place two clubs or two 2" X 4" boards parallel on the floor, slightly wider than the width of your putter. Move the putter back and forth between the club or boards.
- Feel the club, arms, and hands move as a unit.
- Check to see if the blade is square, back and through.
- Back, through, and hold.
- Distance back equals distance through.

Objective 3

To feel the motion of the stroke and hear the differences in contact points on the club (Figure 3.26).

Drills

1. Make ten strokes, hitting the ball on the centroid.
- Check your finish.
- Listen for the sound of contact.

2. Make five strokes, hitting the ball with the toe of the club.
- Listen for the sound of contact.

3. Make five strokes, hitting the ball with the heel of the club.
- Listen for the sound of contact.

4. Make five strokes, hitting the ball on the centroid.
- What is the difference in sound?
- Can you detect a difference in feel?

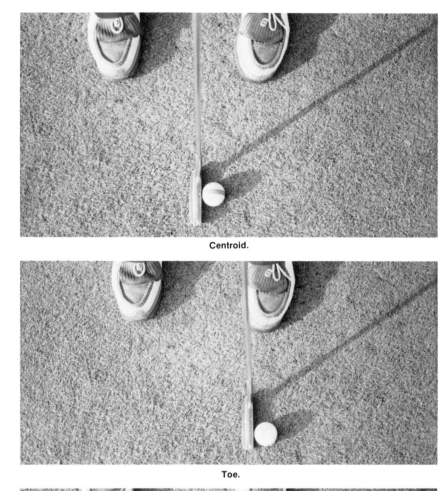

Centroid.

Toe.

Heel.

Figure 3.26. Center and off-center contact affects distance and direction.

Objective 4

To feel the difference in swing length.

Place a 12″-long piece of tape on the floor or carpet, 3 feet from the wall. Place a second strip of tape perpendicular to and at the middle of the long strip. At 2″ intervals from the middle strip to either end, place perpendicular strips (Figure 3.27). Place a piece of tape on the wall in line with the tape. Place the boards or clubs on either side, putter-width apart.

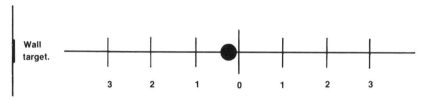

Figure 3.27. Tape provides a good teaching aid for path, face, and swing length.

Drills

1. Practice making strokes 1-to-1, 2-to-2, and 3-to-3.
  - Check your blade on the lines on the backswing and forward swing.

2. Hit balls on the line directed toward the target.
  - Back, through, and hold.
  - Check your blade.

3. Remove the boards or clubs and hit balls, using the line as a guide.

4. Move away from the line and practice your stroke.

5. Hit balls toward a wall target without guides. Vary your stroke from 1-to-1, 2-to-2, and 3-to-3.

Objective 5

To become aware of the stroke length and distance factor.

Drills

1. Ladder Drill — Figure 3.28 illustrates the setup for the Ladder Drill. Line up five clubs, 3 feet apart. Stand to the side and 5 feet from the first club. Putt six balls. Your objective is to putt each ball so that it stops between any two clubs of your choice. For example, putt to the farthest two clubs, then the closest, the middle, etc.

Figure 3.28. The Ladder Drill is used for practicing distance.

2. Clock Drill — Stand in the middle of a practice green. Putt six balls in different directions. Your objective is to putt the ball as close to the fringe as you can.

3. Cluster Drill — Putt three balls. Putt the first ball outside your peripheral vision. Without looking to see the distance, putt the next two, trying to repeat the feel of the stroke. Your objective is to have the balls roll the same distance, forming a cluster.

4. Tee Drill — Putt balls to tees. The tees are smaller than the hole and require greater accuracy and feel (Figure 3.29).

66

Figure 3.29. The Tee Drill is good for distance and accuracy putting practice.

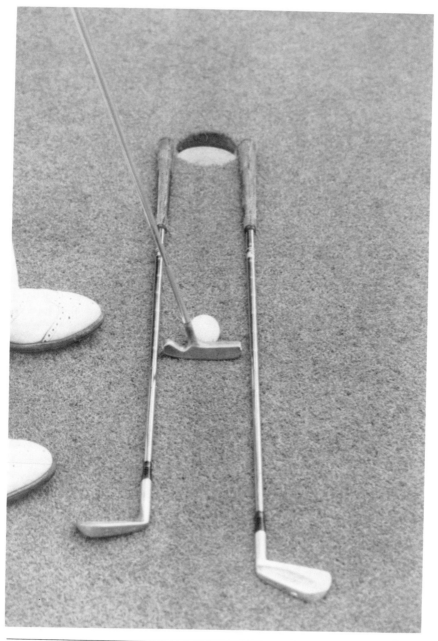

Figure 3.30. The Track Drill develops a feeling for path.

5. Track Drill — Practice putting to a hole through a club track as used indoors (Figure 3.30).

Figure 3.31. The Line Drill develops a compact stroke.

Objective 6

To become aware of target orientation.

1. Line Drill— Place four balls in a line from the hole, 3″ apart (Figure 3.31). Putt the closest ball to the hole, and continue until all the balls have been hit into the hole. When a ball is not holed, replace it and all the balls and begin again. Your objective is to hole all the balls five times in a row.

69

| Target hand. | Rear hand. |

Figure 3.32. One-armed drills develop a sense of stroke control.

2. Circle Drill—Place six balls in a 3-foot circle around the hole. Begin at any ball and putt around the hole.

3. Alternate Circle Drill—Place balls at various distances around the hole. Alternate putting long and short putts.

Additional Putting Drills

1. One-Armed Drills—Practice putting with both your target and rear arms independently (Figure 3.32). Practice at home and on the green.

2. Grip Down Drill—Grip down on the club as illustrated in Figure 3.33. Maintain this position with the shaft against the target arm. If the shaft moves away from your arm, as illustrated in the third figure, your hands have been too active.

Setup.

Forward swing.

Active hands.

Figure 3.33. The Grip Down Drill helps you to feel an arm-hand unit in putting.

71

SAND SHOTS

Sand shots are the unneeded nemesis for many golfers. Actually they are the easiest shots in golf because they are the only shots in which you do not have to hit the ball first! Your swing displaces the sand and the ball rides out with the displaced sand.

Whenever possible, it is highly recommended that a sand wedge be used for this shot. A sand wedge is a utility club specifically designed for use in the sand. The wide and slightly extended downward portion of the club is called the flange. It allows the club to sweep or "bounce" through the sand without going too deep.

Sand wedges vary in the degree of bounce and weight, as well as in design (Figure 3.34). A variety of sand wedge designs (e.g. more or less bounce) are needed because of their effectiveness in different sand textures. If you play on courses that have white, fluffy, light sand, you need a sand wedge with a good bounce. Conversely, a club with low bounce is recommended for courses that have heavier, coarse sand. A high-bounce club in coarse sand tends to cause a shot to scull or thin hit. A low-bounce club in fluffy sand produces a different action. Often, sand wedge designs that are mismatched with sand texture are the culprits for poor sand shots.

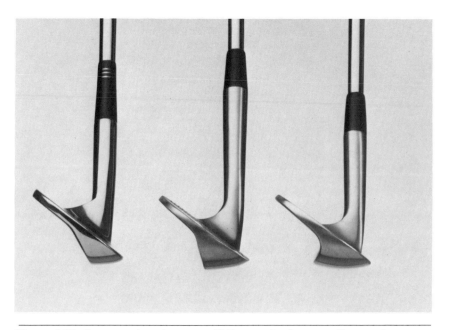

Figure 3.34. Some wedges bounce off the sand, whereas others cut through the sand (left tends to cut, right tends to bounce).

There are two types of sand shots, which are determined by the lie of the ball (Figure 3.35). When the ball is on the surface of the sand and in a good lie, a variety of shots are possible. The basic shot used is called an explosion shot. This shot uses a shallow angle of approach with a sweeping action. The ball comes out with a high, soft trajectory. If the ball is below the level of the sand, your options are reduced. The angle of approach must be steeper, creating more descent. The ball leaves the sand at a lower trajectory and with more roll.

The best way to initially approach the sand shot is to use your regular full-swing motion with a sand wedge. As you progress, modifications can be made to produce a greater variety of shots. But for the present, develop confidence getting out of the sand and onto the green somewhere.

Initially, to execute the sand shot from a good lie on the surface of the sand, maintain your regular full-swing motion. Allow the swing motion to displace the sand and the ball. To do this, the following setup is suggested. As you take your stance in the sand, dig your toes into the sand. This positions your toes below your heels in the sand. Try to slightly dig in the inside of your rear foot. The sand tends to reduce your stability as you swing. This procedure provides greater

Figure 3.35. Balls that land in the sand may bury, whereas others rest on top of the sand.

stability and helps you maintain a better posture over the ball. It also allows the club to enter the sand as a result of the swing motion. Your weight is evenly distributed between both feet.

The club should be slightly open to allow the bounce of the club to contact the sand before the leading edge. This prevents a digging action. The club face should be opened slightly and then gripped, rather than the normal sequence of gripping the club first.

The ball position will be one to two inches to the target side of center. It will vary slightly with the distance you want the ball to go. For example, you will take more sand when the ball is forward of center, producing a shorter distance shot. The ball position for your particular swing will be determined through practice.

The explosion shot produces a fairly high trajectory. When it lands, it has minimum roll. The ball below the surface of the sand may be buried with only a small portion of the ball in view, in an oval caused by its impact with the sand ("fried egg"), or in a footprint. Whatever its location, some portion of the ball is below the surface of the sand. This type of lie requires a slight modification in your normal setup. It is similar to the mini-swing setup, with a longer swing motion.

When you have a good lie, move the ball position to the rear side of center. This helps to create a descending angle of approach, which drives the sand more forward than up. The club must go deeper through the sand to propel the ball out.

The clubface is delofted, as opposed to the slightly open clubface of the explosion shot. The difference in the lie of the shot and entering angle of approach necessitates the change. A buried lie hit with an open clubface at a shallow angle could bury the ball more or produce other less desirable results.

The weight setup is with the toes below the heels and to the inside of the rear foot. This is the same setup as in the explosion shot. Initially, set the weight evenly between your feet. As you practice, you may want to alter this position slightly, with more weight to the target side. This shot, due to the lie and necessary ball position, produces a low trajectory with a lot of roll.

The key to developing good sand play is to swing through the sand, not at the sand. The sand displaces the ball. Too often, an attempt to get the ball out of the trap results in trying to lift the ball out with your hands. This causes the swing motion to stop at the ball or to catch the top part of the ball, sending it flying over the green.

Think of yourself splashing water in a swimming pool or lake. The sand reacts the same way as the water. If you take your fist and hit straight down through the water, a spout goes up. If the same motion were made but your fist stopped at the water, the splash would be minimal. When the club stops in the sand, only some sand is displaced and the ball moves a short distance, if at all.

To understand varying the trajectory of the sand shot, expand the splashing analogy. If you are standing next to a friend and you want to hit the friend in the face with water, you automatically swing your hand and arm into the water at a high or steep angle. The water goes up into the face at the same angle your hand entered the water. If that same friend were farther away, your hand and arm would enter the water at a shallower angle. The water would travel at a lower trajectory, covering a greater distance. In both cases the hand and arm swing through the water.

Now apply this analogy to sand. The higher the ball needs to go, the steeper the angle away from the ball on the backswing and return on the forward swing. The longer sand shot requires a shallower approach, similar to the regular swing.

SAND SHOT PRACTICE SUGGESTIONS

As you begin to practice sand shots, notice differences in the sand. If you are fortunate enough to play courses with contrasting sand textures, feel the differences. Pick up a handful of sand at the different courses on which you play and feel the texture of the sand. The coarse sand is rough and gritty. The soft sand is smooth and fine. Note the differences as you stand in the sand. The soft sand is less stable and usually has a thicker base. Your feet go deeper into the sand when you take your stance. There is a color difference. Coarse sand is darker, sometimes dirty in appearance, while the softer, silica sand is whiter and has a crystal-like appearance.

An awareness of these differences will help you determine the type of shot to expect in different textures, how much sand to displace for different distances, and the most effective sand wedge to use. With a better understanding of the sand, you will gradually become more comfortable.

The practice suggestions are presented progressively in a step-by-step manner. If you already feel comfortable in the sand, this progression provides a good review of basic concepts.

Work through Objectives 1-6 and the accompanying drills with the ball in a good lie. Try to establish a 75% to 80% success rate prior to moving to the next step. Rake the trap frequently to assure a good lie. Then repeat taking the setup position for a ball below the surface of the sand. Note the differences in ball trajectory and the amount of roll compared to the height for each type of shot. This will help you plan your landing areas on the courses you play.

Objective 1

To develop a feel for the sand wedge and bounce effect of the sole. A sand wedge with some degree of bounce is suggested. These drills are practiced out of the sand.

Drills

1. Make five practice swings with your sand wedge.

2. Make five practice swings with your 9-iron.
- Can you feel a difference between the two clubs in the weight of the head?

3. Repeat drills 1 and 2 with your eyes closed.
- Can you detect a difference?
- Close your eyes and have a friend give you one of the two clubs without telling you which it is. Can you detect the difference in feel by swinging it?

4. Open the face of your sand wedge and grip the club. Make five practice swings, brushing the ground through a selected point.
- Can you feel the bounce effect as you swing?

5. Square the face of the sand wedge and grip the club. Make five practice swings, brushing the ground through a selected point.
- Can you feel a difference between the open and square blade as you brush the ground?
- Can you hear a difference as you brush the ground?

Objective 2

To develop a feel of the different setup position in the sand.

Drills

1. Take your normal full-swing stance, with your feet level in the sand. Make five practice swings.
- Where did you contact the sand? Center? Back of center? Forward of center?

2. Take the suggested sand stance, with your toes dug in below the level of your heels and the inside of your rear foot below the outside (Figure 3.36). Make practice swings.
- Where did you contact the ball? Center? Back of center? Forward of center?

3. Take your normal full-swing stance and dig your heels in below your toes(opposite of drill 2). Make five practice swings.
- Where did you contact the sand? Center? Back of center? Forward of center?
- Which of the three stances provided the best stability with upper and lower body motion?

76

Figure 3.36. The relationship between the level of your toes and your heels may be critical. This golfer has his toes lower than his heels.

Objective 3

To develop an understanding of the differences in sand displacement between an open and delofted clubface.

Drills

Take the suggested sand setup position, with your toes below your heels.

1. Make five practice swings with an open face. (Note: Open the club face, then grip the club.)
   - How much sand was displaced?
   - Was the angle of entry steep or shallow?

2. Make five practice swings with clubface delofted.
   - How much sand was displaced?
   - Was the angle of entry steep or shallow?

77

Figure 3.37. The ball rides out on the sand, displaced by hitting through the line.

Figure 3.38. A good visual image for a short shot is to imagine the ball as the yolk of an egg. Swing through the entire egg in order to throw it out of the bunker.

Objective 4

To develop a swing feel for contacting the sand at one point.

Drills

Draw a line in the sand, as illustrated in Figure 3.37. Place the line in the center of your stance. Open the clubface slightly and grip the club.

1. Make practice swings, moving along the line. Displace sand from the line forward, toward the target. Sand displacement should be shallow, not deep.
   - Where are you contacting the sand? On the line, forward, or back of the line?

2. Adjust the line to the position in which you contacted the sand 75% of the time during your practice swings. Make ten practice swings, displacing the sand from the line toward the target.
   - Where are you contacting the sand? On the line, forward, or back of the line?

3. Draw five ovals in the sand (Figure 3.38). Displace the sand from the ovals.

79

Objective 5

To displace the sand, knocking the ball out of the trap with a line and oval. The ball should have a good lie.

Draw a line approximately 36 inches long in the sand, as illustrated in Figure 3.37.

The line will extend away from you and be positioned in your stance at the low point of your arc. Halfway up the line, place six balls, spaced 3 inches apart along the line and 1 inch on the target side of the line.

Drills

1. Start swinging back and forth, and displace sand from the line forward, toward the target.
  - How many balls did you knock out of the sand?
  - Repeat until all six go out of the sand.

2. Repeat the last half of drill 1, with the balls in front of the line.
  - How many balls did you knock out?
  - Repeat until all six go out of the sand.

3. Draw six ovals in the sand as previously illustrated. Place the ball on the target side of the oval. Displace the sand from the oval.
  - How many balls went out of the trap?
  - Repeat until all six balls go out of the trap.

Objective 6

To knock the ball out of the trap with a good lie.

Drills

Place ten balls in trap. Make sure each ball has a good lie (such as on the surface of the sand).

1. For each shot, take your setup position for the sand. Direct your swing toward a target.
  - How many balls did you knock out of the sand?
  - How many balls remained on the green?

2. Repeat until eight balls are successfully knocked out of the trap and remain on the green.

On the Course

From your practice sessions, you have developed an understanding and feel for getting out of the sand. As you play, your major goal is to get out of the sand. Right now, anywhere on the green is desirable. However, there may be times when you will want to chip out of the

Figure 3.39. "To try or not to try" is often the question.

sand going away from the green, then go for the green. Retreat may be the better part of valor! Even for the finest players, it is not always advisable to go for the pin. Gallant intentions have ruined many scores (Figure 3.39).

The following situations often arise, and you must decide which is the best choice of actions.

Situation A

The ball is buried on the back slope of the trap. A big overhanging lip is on the target side of the green. Go for it or retreat?

- Retreat—A buried lie will come out low and the odds of rolling it up and over the lip are slim. Select the safest exit route from the trap.

Situation B

The ball is in a flat trap 4 feet from the green edge of the trap. The lie is good and the fringe is low. The pin is 15 feet away. Explosion shot or putt?

- This is an ideal situation to putt. It is the safest and most controlled shot for accuracy and distance.

Situation C

The ball is buried in the incline slope of the green side of the trap. The pin is 10 feet away. Retreat or go for it?

- This usually appears to be a tough shot. The sand will help propel the ball upward and propel it quickly. Make the same swing and setup as for the buried lie. Be sure to swing through and pull upward. The ball pops right out and pops out softly.

Summary

When you are inexperienced in the sand, it is not uncommon to be uncomfortable and anxious. You are not alone in your feelings. Keep practicing. Trust your swing motion to help you. It may take a while to develop that confidence, but have patience. Remember, it is not necessary to get fancy, just *get out.*

4

ADVANCED SWING TECHNIQUES

In order to understand as well as execute the more advanced shots, it is critical that you understand the golf swing and are able to consistently execute the basic swing techniques. Very few individuals can learn to run before they can walk. The same principle is true in golf. The basics must be mastered before the advanced shots can be attempted.

Full-swing and short-game techniques will be illustrated in this section. These provide application of pace control (e.g. 1/2 and 3/4 swings of various distances), face control (e.g. intentional hooking and slicing), variations in trajectory (e.g. high and low shots), and challenge shots (e.g. uphill and downhill lies and tree shots). Practice techniques will be provided with each of these real-life applications.

PACE CONTROL

Swing pace is the controllable speed of the swing. The pace may be slow or fast, depending on the desired distance. To understand and control pace you need to be aware of the "swing pacers."

Try this drill without a ball: Holding an iron, take your normal full-swing posture. Place your rear foot directly behind your target-side foot. Be sure to place only the toe of the rear foot on the ground, as indicated in Figure 4.1.

83

Figure 4.1. The Toe Drill demonstration, correct positive position, and placement of the rear foot.

Maintaining that position, try the following exercises. (Note: Exercises 1-4 may be done inside. Exercises 5-12 should be done on the practice tee.)

1. Make a one-lever -half swing (3-to-3 swing length) with your arms, hands, and club moving as one unit. Repeat this swing several times.
    *   What is the swing sensation of this motion?

2. Without moving your arms from the extended position at address, cock and uncock your wrist. Be sure that you have a full wrist cock on the backswing and forward swing (Figure 4.2). Repeat several times.
    *   What sensation do you feel in your hands?
    *   What is the difference in sensation between Exercise 1 and Exercise 2?

Figure 4.2. The Cocking Drill demonstrates a full-wrist clock on the backswing and forward swing.

85

3. Incorporate an arm swing with the hand action created by the cocking and uncocking of the wrist. This becomes a two-lever motion. Repeat several times.
- What is the swing sensation of this motion?
- What is the swing sensation difference between the one-half swing and the no-swing with full cock?
- What is the swing sensation of this exercise compared to Exercise 2? Which had no arm action?

4. Incorporate lower-body motion with weight shift. This requires a normal stance with both feet parallel. Repeat several times.
- What is the swing sensation of this motion?
- What is the swing sensation of this exercise compared to Exercise 3? Which had no lower-body action?

5-8. Repeat Exercises 1-4, hitting a teed ball with a 7-iron, and using your normal stance and setup. Make several swings to establish a normal swing pace.
- What are the results with a normal swing pace (3)? Slower swing pace (1 or 2)? Faster swing pace (4 or 5)?
- What are the differences in swing sensation and corresponding distance results?

9-12. Repeat Exercises 5-8, using your upper body to increase speed.
- What are the differences in swing feel and results when your shoulders exert too much influence, contrasted to Exercises 5-8?

There is a reason for each of these exercises. Each should relate a different sensation of motion and speed. By isolating the arm swing with speed in the hands created by the cocking and uncocking of the wrist. The change in stance from one leg back to a normal stance will allow for addition of the lower body, providing a wider base of support and greater arm swing and hand action.

Referring to the LPP Model, the levering action incorporated in the arms-only swing motion is a one-lever system. Distance potential is limited. However, this one-lever system has its advantages in improved accuracy with a shorter length swing, as in the mini-swings.

The wrist action of the cocking and uncocking motion produces a two-lever system. Isolating the wrist action with no arm swing produces enough speed to propel the ball a fair distance. When the arm swing is added, the distance potential increases. It can be further increased by adding the lower-body motion.

Basically, in the swing motion, the arms produce the swing motion about the swing center and the hands transmit the speed through sequential timing of the body action and the levering system. Therefore, the swing pacers in the swing are: the arms, which supply the swing motion; the hands, which transmit the speed; and the body and legs, which provide the foundation and support system for the swing motion.

These drills will allow you to apply the following principles to the swing motion: levering system (one and two levers), width of arc (target arm extension), length of arc (1-to-1, 2-to-2, 3-to-3), balance (static to dynamic), width of stance (foot width and shoulder width), timing (no release to timed release), and swing center (stationary to moving). From experiencing the drills and variations in the swing principles, you should now have a better conceptual and practical understanding of pace control and "swing pacers."

Practice Application

Pace control is important in all facets of the game. No one who swings at 100% on every shot is capable of playing good golf. Doing so would be extremely fatiguing. Besides, it is not possible within the demands of the game, and swing control would deteriorate quickly.

Different shots require a variation in feel and sensitivity to different playing conditions. The same type of shot within a round may require a different feel for distance. Green conditions often vary on a course. Weather conditions often change during a round. You change. Therefore, one swing pace will not suffice during an entire round.

To learn pace control requires practice, developing a feel for what suits you best. If you tend to move slowly in your everyday activities, you will probably tend toward a slow pace in your golf swing. Your golf game will tend to reflect your personality. Realizing this, you can learn to work with yourself rather than against your natural instincts.

Pace control can be learned by practicing, using the pendulum concept presented in the short-game techniques. In this concept, swing length is controlled by an awareness of arm swing. The following Cluster Drills are designed to develop an understanding of pace relative to the length of the swing and variations in speed controlled by the arms and hands. For each pace and swing length, the struck balls should cluster at a particular location in the fairway (Figure 4.3).

During each of your practice sessions, try to accomplish one of the following objectives, beginning with the first one. If you are able to accomplish more than one at a session, that is fine. However, each new objective requires the foundation of the previous one. Initially use an 8- or 9-iron. You will be able to use most of your clubs as you develop a sense of pace. You should continue to practice each drill until you establish an 80% or better consistency rate.

87

Figure 4.3. The Cluster Drill helps establish pace control for different distances.

Objective 1

To become more aware of your ability to control your arms through various lengths (1-to-1, 2-to-2, 3-to-3, 4-to-4, 5-to-5).

Drills

Make ten swings of each swing length from the recommended setup positions for the one-lever swings two-lever swings. Note: Using the word key "back-through" hold your ending so that you can check the length of your forward swing. Relate the length of the backswing to the length of the forward swing.

1. Without a ball—Visually match the feel of each swing with the lengths at each position (1-to-1 through 5-to-5).

2. Eyes closed without a ball—Establish the same feel as with your eyes open (1-to-1 through 5-to-5).

3. With a ball placed on a tee—Match the distance the ball travels with the associated swing length and feel (1-to-1 through 5-to-5). The balls should begin to form clusters at distances matched to swing lengths.

4. With a ball (not teed)—Match the distance the ball travels with the associated swing length and feel. The balls should begin to form clusters at distances matched to swing lengths.

5. With a ball in a divot (or stepped on)—Match the distance the ball travels with the associated swing length and feel. The balls should begin to form clusters at distances matched to swing lengths.

88

Objective 2

To be able to vary the pace of the swing (normal, slow, fast).

Drill

Make ten swings of each swing length from the recommended setup positions, varying your swing pace from slow to normal to fast. Consider these paces as 1-5, with normal being a 3.

1. Without a ball — Feel the change of pace within any one swing length as you move from slow (1) to fast (5). Try it at each swing length (1-to-1 through 5-to-5).
2. Without a ball and with eyes closed—Try to establish the same feel as with your eyes open. Vary both the swing length and speed of swing.
3. With a ball placed on a tee—Match the distance the ball travels with the associated swing length and speed changes. Experiment with longer swings (5) at slow paces (1) and shorter swings (1) at fast paces (5). With each swing length and speed, the balls should begin to form clusters at distances matched to swing length and pace differences.
4. With a ball (not teed)—Match the distance the ball travels with the associated swing length and speed changes. Experiment with longer swings (5) at slow paces (1) and shorter swings (1) at fast paces (5). With each swing length and speed, the balls should begin to form clusters at distances matched to swing length and pace differences.
5. With a ball in a divot—match the distance the ball travels with the associated swing length and speed changes. Experiment with longer swings (5) at slow paces (1) and shorter swings (1) at fast paces (5). With each swing length and speed, the balls should begin to form clusters at distances matched to swing length and pace differences.

Objective 3

To be able to relate and execute different swing lengths and pace for the same distance. Note: Walk off distances of 10, 20, 30, 40, and 50 yards if they are not already marked at the practice facility. Place a marker at each yardage point.

Drill

Make ten swings for each swing length and pace for each distance.
1. Without a ball—Looking at each distance marker, make swings, visually matching the associated feel with the desired distance.

2. With a ball—Match the distance the ball travels with the associated swing length, and feel pace changes for the desired distance. With each distance, you should begin to identify the swing length and pace that you can best execute.

3. With a ball in a divot—Match the distance the ball travels with the associated swing length, and feel pace changes for the desired distance. With each distance, you should begin to identify the swing length and pace that you can best execute.

Objective 4

To be able to relate and execute different swing lengths and pace for a variety of distances. Note: From the previous drills, you have been developing a visual match of related distances and a feel for pace and swing lengths. This drill is closer to actual on-course situations.

Drill

Identify targets of various lengths (known and unknown) within your ability to reach with the club(s) of your choice. Alternating close and distant targets, and using the same and different clubs, execute the shot required after predetermining your swing length and pace. Match the distance the ball travels with the associated swing length and pace changes for the desired distances. With practice, your pace control and selection should allow you to execute this drill at a fairly high success rate.

Course Application

As you begin to feel the differences in swing length and pace, your ability to score will improve. You will make better shot selections, club selections, and shot executions.

The following examples are typical on-course situations during which pace control must be considered. As you think about these situations, remember that pace control is specific to you as an individual. You must know your shot execution abilities and you must be able to respond to how you feel at any particualr moment. There are no right or wrong responses to these situations. You must experiment with all responses and then select your preference.

1. It is early in the round and you feel sluggish. You have left your approach shots with irons on the front edge of two greens.
Options:
- Hit one more club than you think you need with the same swing pace.
- Hit the club you normally need, increasing swing pace.

90

2. It is toward the end of the round. You are leading the tournament by three shots. You feel strong and have been aggressive. You have been taking one less club than normal. You are forced with an approach shot into a well-trapped green with a front pin placement.

Options:
- Hit one less club than you think you need with the same swing pace.
- Hit the club you normally need, decreasing swing pace.

3. You are playing in windy conditions. You have a 9-iron approach shot with a tail wind.

Options:
- Hit one less club with the same swing pace.
- Hit one more club, decreasing swing pace and swing length.
- Hit the same club with the same swing pace and less swing length.
- Hit the same club, decreasing swing pace.

4. You have been practicing putting on slow greens. You go to a course with extremely fast greens.

Options:
- Decrease swing length with the same swing pace.
- Decrease swing pace with the same swing length.
- Decrease swing length and swing pace.

5. You have played most of the round on fairly fast greens. There is a heavy rain. When play is continued, the greens are extremely slow.

Options:
- Increase in swing pace with the same swing length.
- Increase swing length with the same swing pace.
- Increase swing length and swing pace.

6. You are playing into a head wind. You have a 7-iron approach shot into the green with no trouble in front.

Options:
- Hit a 7-iron with an increase in swing pace.
- Hit a 6-iron with the same swing pace.
- Hit a 5-iron with a shorter (4-to-4) swing length and the same swing pace.

From these situations, you can see that the conditions of the course, the weather, and your awareness level influence pace and the variations needed during specific rounds, or from one round or day to another. Incorporating pace control into your practice sessions and developing a higher awareness of pace control during play will enhance your scoring ability.

FACE CONTROL

The position of the clubface at impact is one of the five factors affecting ball flight (LPP Model). How the clubface hits the ball determines how the ball will curve in flight. As the ball begins to slow down, the curvature is seen as the direction the ball curves off the flight path (Figure 4.4).

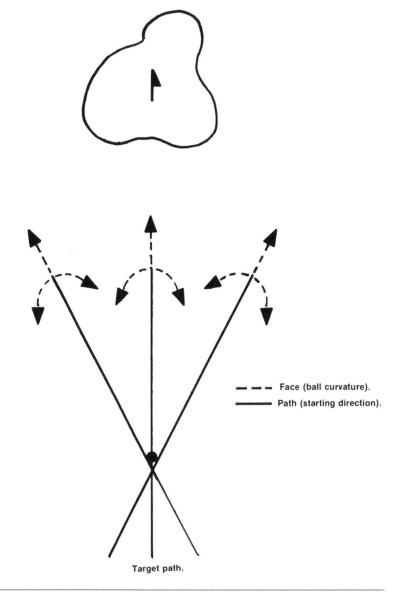

- - - Face (ball curvature).
——— Path (starting direction).

Target path.

Figure 4.4. Nine possible ball flights with indicated curvature.

The three positions of the clubface at impact are open, square, and closed. These are illustrated in Figure 4.5 with the corresponding curvature produced. For the right-handed player, an open clubface produces a left-to-right ball flight curvature, which is noted as a fade or slice. A square clubface produces a relatively straight ball flight. A closed clubface produces a right-to-left ball flight curvature, noted as a draw or hook. The degree that the clubface is opened or closed at impact determines the degree of curvature.

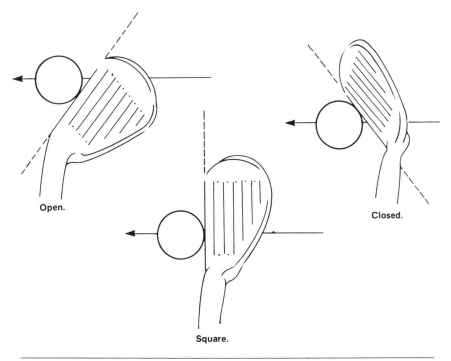

Figure 4.5. Clubface position affecting ball flight curvature.

The hands control the position of the clubface at impact. Numerous factors within the swing motion can influence the position of the hands at impact and corresponding variations in the clubface positions. Some of these may be desirable, others less desirable. The intent of this section will be to focus on ways to intentionally vary the ball flight curvature.

There are two basic ways to intentionally vary ball flight curvature. The first and perhaps most common is to alter the grip position. The second is to alter the grip pressure in the hands. Both of these influence curvature by either activating or deactivating hand action.

The grip positions illustrated in Chapter 3 allow the hands to operate differently during the swing. The neutral grip (palms of both hands facing each other with two knuckles visible) permits efficient hand action to return the club squarely to the ball while using a free-arm swing. This position is usually suggested first.

The "hooking grip" has the palms of both hands facing each other. The target hand is more on top of the club, the rear hand more under. Three or four knuckles are visible on the target hand. This tends to encourage activating the hand action and closing the blade through impact, creating a hook curvature.

The "slicing grip," as do the other two grip positions, has the palms of both hands facing each other. The hand positions are reversed from the "hook grip." The target hand moves more under the club, the rear hand is more on top. Three or four knuckles are visible on the rear hand. This position tends to deactivate the hand action through impact, creating a slice curvature.

As the hands move away from a neutral position—as a unit, in either direction, on top of the club, or under the club—a change in clubface at impact occurs. The degree of change from neutral influences the degree of curvature, depending upon your individual hand action.   The second method of influencing ball flight curvature is through grip pressure. Pressure points are the last three fingers of both hands. Grip pressure is individual. There is no way to measure its exactness, only its effectiveness. Grip pressure affects the tension level in the hands and has two related effects—it influences hand action and muscle tension in the arms and shoulders. A 1-to-5 pressure scale can be applied, with 1 representing little to no pressure and absence of control and 5 representing too much pressure and overcontrol. Extremes in either direction are undesirable.

Through practice, you develop a fairly constant grip pressure. This is usually indicated by a consistent ball flight direction or path, and ball flight curvature. Ideally, this curvature will be no more than a fade or draw.

By increasing or decreasing your grip pressure, you can change the ball flight curvature. An extreme pressure (5) produces excessive tension in the hands, which reduces hand action. This extreme pressure creates the majority of slices by ineffective and insufficient hand action or release through the ball. The reverse is true at the opposite extreme (1), with too little tension producing some hooks. As you practice, you will be able to determine the optimal pressure for your swing needs.

Up to this point, ball flight curvature has been related to shots that have been on line to a given target, with the end ball flight curving to the right or left. Often there are times in which a straight line direction

Hook.

Slice.

Figure 4.6. Hitting around trees requires intentional curving of the ball flight.

95

is not possible, as when hitting the ball around trees (Figure 4.6). This requires implementing the same principles with an adjustment in alignment.

The following steps are suggested if you wish to intentionally curve a ball:

- Align your clubface toward the intended target.
- Align your body parallel to the intended ball path (the direction in which you want the ball to start).
- Make your regular swing.

Practice Application

As you practice and begin to groove your swing, you will develop a consistent ball flight curvature. This is based on a methodical approach in which sound basic fundamentals are stressed. A constant grip and grip pressure are important aspects of those basic fundamentals. Your hands are the communication link in your swing. Your grip and grip pressure become the basic language of your swing. You can never overpractice your grip. You must be able to establish the grip you desire.

To guide your practice efficiency, place a club on the ground as a directional line. The club will point slightly to the right of your target, but this will allow your ball to be on the target line. Place the ball about four inches from the club, with your stance parallel to the club. This assures you of consistent alignment.

The following suggestions for practicing ball flight curvature will provide you with a systematic approach that can be fun and motivating. You should continue to implement objectives to direct your practice sessions. As you practice pace control, work on one objective at a time. You should try to develop an 80% or better consistency rate.

Objective 1

To become more aware of the effects of grip changes in altering ball flight curvature.

Drill

Hit twenty balls with a 5-iron toward a selected target. Chart the ball fight curvature, using Table 4.1 as a guide.

- What percentage did you hit with each curvature? Note: If your consistency rate was not at least 70% with one of the three, it is suggested that, as you go through the drills, you try to establish a grip position and pressure that can help you establish a minimal consistency rate of 70% to 80%.

Table 4.1

This chart is a guideline for developing an awareness of your ball flight tendencies.

Curvature	Shots																				Total	%
	1	2	3	4	5	6	7	8	9	10	11	12	13	14	15	16	17	18	19	20		
Left	L	L	L	L	L	L	L	L	L	L	L	L	L	L	L	L	L	L	L	L		
Straight	S	S	S	S	S	S	S	S	S	S	S	S	S	S	S	S	S	S	S	S		
Right	R	R	R	R	R	R	R	R	R	R	R	R	R	R	R	R	R	R	R	R		

Steps:

1. Circle the curvature for each shot.
2. Add the total for each curvature.
3. Determine the percentage.

97

Objective 2

To become more aware of the effects of grip changes in altering ball flight curvature.

Drill

Make ten full swings with each grip position (neutral, hook, slice) toward a selected target.

1. Without hitting a ball—Visually match the grip position with the associated feel as you swing.
2. Without a ball and with your eyes closed—Establish the same feel as with your eyes open.
3. With a ball placed on a tee—Match the curvature of the ball with the associated grip position.
4. With a ball (not teed)—Match the curvature of the ball with the associated grip position.

Objective 3

To be able to vary the curvature of the ball flight to a selected target by changing grip positions.

Drill

Alternate hook, slice, and neutral grip positions on twenty-one shots toward a selected target.

Objective 4

To be able to alter your alignment slightly in order to have the curvature of the ball fall in the direction of the desired target. Note: Remove the alignment club.

Drill

Change your alignment with each grip change to allow for the ball to fall toward the target. Continue to alternate among hook, slice, and neutral positions.

Objective 5

To become more aware of how grip pressure changes alter ball flight curvature of the ball fall in the direction of the desired target. (Note: Remove the alignment club.)

Drill

Make ten full swings with your normal grip pressure (3), extreme pressure (5), and very light pressure (1).

1. Without a ball—Note the differences in the mobility of your hands.
2. With a ball placed on a tee—Match the curvature of the ball with the associated changes in grip pressure.
3. With a ball (not teed)—Match the curvature of the ball with the associated changes in grip pressure.

From the drills, you may have discovered several things about your grip and grip pressure. Your normal grip may have been either too much on top or too far under the club, causing erratic or undesirable curvature. You may have found that your normal grip pressure was either too light or—what is generally the case—too tight. Extremes in either direction are limiting in developing consistency and control.

The extreme grip changes will allow you to develop the feeling of the activation and deactivation of the hands that the grip position permits. Continue to practice in the extremes to find the middle area for your best grip.

You will find that the grip changes will provide for extremes in curvature often needed on the course. If you need to hook or slice the ball dramatically, you may need to adjust your grip position. For the subtle changes in ball curvature needed for a slight draw or fade coming into greens, grip pressure changes should provide the needed curvature. These pressure changes also keep the shot from getting away in either direction on tee shots. You will probably find that you either hook or slice more easily. This tendency to either hook or slice is based on the characteristics of your individual swing. However, it is important that you learn to execute draws and fades as well as hooks and slices.

Course Application

The ability to control ball flight curvature provides greater flexibility in your game. Often, curving the ball in one direction or the other can provide the difference in an opportunity for a birdie vs. a potential bogey.

From your practice session you should be aware of your natural curve tendency. Whenever possible, you should allow for it. The less you have to maneuver the ball, the less anxious the situation becomes.

The following course situations are times you may want to consider maneuvering the ball. As with the situations in pace control there are no right or wrong responses. These are presented for consideration. You must continue to become more aware of your present abilities and areas in which to improve. Your response at this time may change later, or on different days, or within a given round.

Situations

1. The hole is a par 4 with a dogleg left. The dogleg begins about 185 yards off the tee. You tend to slice your driver.
Options:
- Play your normal tee shot.
- Try to draw your tee shot.

Thoughts:
Determine what the percentages are that you can draw the drive. How many previous times have you been successful? If you have been successful only a limited number of times, mental pressure is increased as well as grip pressure. Both work against a successful draw. If you are comfortable drawing the ball, this would be the better shot.

2. You have a 7-iron approach shot to the green. The pin is tucked on the right side of the green behind a trap. Your normal shot is a slight draw (right-handed golfer).

Options:
- Hit your normal shot at the pin.
- Hit your normal shot to the middle of the green.
- Hit a slight fade toward the middle of the green.

Thoughts:
The tight pin placement is the major consideration. Traps are often tension creators for many golfers. During the round, how precise have your previous shots been to the pin? What is the importance of the shot? Can you fade the ball easily? (This is a situation that, with a feel for changing grip pressure to produce curvature, would enhance your ability to get close.)

3. Your ball is twenty yards behind a tree that is between you and the pin. The tree is too high to go over and too low to go under. Your ball is in the left rough with a wide fairway to the right and 140 yards from the green. You tend to hook.

Options:
- Chip out.
- Hook around the tree.

Thoughts:
This is a case where your natural tendencies can work to your advantage for getting out of a trouble situation. The opportunity for success is definitely in your favor. Go for it!

TRAJECTORY CONTROL

Trajectory control is understanding how and when to hit shots higher or lower than the normal trajectory of a given club. The "normal" trajectory of your stroke is determined as you practice and your swing becomes more consistent. In your stance you establish a ball position that is constant for your regular full-swing shots. This position is usually center (or slightly to the target side of center) for full shots with irons and closer to the target foot with woods.

To vary the trajectory, the ball position is altered and you make your regular swing. To hit the ball higher, the ball position is moved closer to the target foot; to hit the ball lower, the ball position is moved closer to the rear foot (Figure 4.7). By altering the ball position, loft is added to the club at impact (forward position) or reduced from the club at impact (back position). When compared to the "normal" shot, the higher trajectory produces less roll, whereas the lower trajectory produces more roll. Both trajectories, high and low, tend to produce less distance than the normal shot.

High trajectory.   **Low trajectory.**

Figure 4.7. To vary the trajectory, the ball position is altered.

101

Practice Application

The practice sessions and objectives presented for trajectory control are intended to help you understand how you can alter ball position for various trajectories, the influence of ball lie on trajectory, and how to modify swing length and pace with ball position to create a wide variety of shots. Each objective builds upon the preceding one. You may, only be able to handle Objectives 1-3, however, as you continue to develop your swing the other objectives will become easier.

In your practice sessions, begin with an iron of your choice. Each drill should, in time, be practiced with both woods and irons. You will find some drills are easier with irons than with woods. Some ball positions will be more effective than others. It is important for you to try all drills with both woods and irons. You will find that, for your particular swing characteristics, you are more effective with certain ball positions. This is the purpose of guided practice.

Objective 1

To develop an awareness of trajectory and roll variations by altering ball position and making your regular full swing.

Drills

1. Hit ten balls from your normal ball position. Note the trajectory and roll.
2. Hit ten balls with the ball positioned off your target foot. Note the trajectory and roll.
3. Hit ten balls with the ball positioned off your rear foot. Note the trajectory and roll.
4. Hit ten balls with the ball positioned midway between your normal ball position and your target foot. Note the trajectory and roll. Compare the trajectory and roll when the ball is played off your target foot vs. from your normal ball position.
5. Hit ten balls with the ball positioned midway between your normal ball position and your rear foot. Note the trajectory and roll. Compare the trajectory and roll when the ball is played off your rear foot vs. from your normal ball position.

Objective 2

To develop an awareness of the distance factor when the trajectory is changed by altering the normal ball position.

Drills

1. Hit ten balls from your normal ball position. Note the trajectory and roll. Note the distance the ball travels.

2. Hit ten balls with the ball positioned off your target foot. Note the trajectory and roll. Note the distance the ball travels.

3. Hit ten balls with the ball positioned off your rear foot. Note the trajectory and roll. Note the distance the ball travels.

4. Hit ten balls with the ball positioned midway between your normal ball position and your target foot. Note the trajectory and roll. Compare the trajectory and roll when the ball is played off your target foot vs. from your normal ball position. Note the distance the ball travels.

5 Hit ten balls with the ball positioned midway between your normal ball position and your rear foot. Note the trajectory and roll. Compare the trajectory and roll when the ball is played off your rear foot vs. from your normal ball position. Note the distance the ball travels.

Objective 3

To develop an awareness of the lie of the ball and trajectory control. For each drill, hit five shots from a good lie and five shots from a bad lie.

Drills

1. Hit ten balls from your normal ball position. Note the trajectory and roll.

2. Hit ten balls with the ball positioned off your target foot. Note the trajectory and roll.

3. Hit ten balls with the ball positioned off your rear foot. Note the trajectory and roll.

4. Hit ten balls with the ball positioned midway between your normal ball position and your target foot. Note the trajectory and roll. Compare the trajectory and roll when the ball is played off your target foot vs. from your normal ball position.

5. Hit ten balls with the ball positioned midway between your normal ball position and your rear foot. Note the trajectory and roll. Compare the trajectory and roll when the ball is played off your rear foot vs. from your normal ball position.

103

Objective 4

To develop an awareness of controlling the distance factor by alternating trajectory and swing length.

For each drill, vary the swing length. Hit shots at your normal full-swing lengths, 3/4 swing, and mini-swings (5-to-5 through 1-to-1).

Drills

1. Hit ten balls from your normal ball position. Note the trajectory and roll. Note the distance the ball travels.
2. Hit ten balls with the ball positioned off your target foot. Note the trajectory and roll. Note the distance the ball travels.
3. Hit ten balls with the ball positioned off your rear foot. Note the trajectory and roll. Note the distance the ball travels.
4. Hit ten balls with the ball positioned midway between your normal ball position and your target foot. Note the trajectory and roll. Compare the trajectory and roll when the ball is played off your target foot vs. from your normal ball position. Note the distance the ball travels.
5. Hit ten balls with the ball positioned midway between your normal ball position and your rear foot. Note the trajectory and roll. Compare the trajectory and roll when the ball is played off your rear foot vs. from your normal ball position. Note the distance the ball travels.

Objective 5

To develop awareness of controlling the distance factor by alternating trajectory and swing space.

For each drill, vary the swing pace. Hit shots at your normal swing pace, faster, and slower.

Drills

1. Hit ten balls from your normal ball position. Note the trajectory and roll. Note the distance the ball travels.
2. Hit ten balls with the ball positioned off your target foot. Note the trajectory and roll. Note the distance the ball travels.
3. Hit ten balls with the ball positioned off your rear foot. Note the trajectory and roll. Note the distance the ball travels.
4. Hit ten balls with the ball positioned midway between your normal ball position and your target foot. Note the trajectory and roll. Compare the trajectory and roll when the ball is played off your target foot vs. from your normal ball position. Note the distance the ball travels.

5. Hit ten balls with the ball positioned midway between your normal ball position and your rear foot. Note the trajectory and roll. Compare the trajectory and roll when the ball is played off your rear foot vs. from your normal ball position. Note the distance the ball travels.

Through your practice sessions of controlling trajectory, you should have discovered that playing the ball nearer your target foot produces a higher trajectory and less roll, whereas playing it toward your rear foot produces a lower ball flight and greater roll. Your eyes should also have become more sensitive to the possible trajectories produced by alternating ball position and using various clubs. This becomes critical as you play and begin to be more creative in your shot selection and execution. You also become more aware of which shots are realistic and which are unrealistic based on the lie of the ball and your ability to cope with the situation.

Course Application

Trajectory control is most often associated with maneuvering over or under trees (Figure 4.8). From your practice sessions on trajectory control and the previous section on face control, a greater selection of shot potentials should be possible.

A good rule of thumb for executing high or low shots on the course is to first determine the ideal club for the needed trajectory. In order to allow a greater margin for error, if height is needed, take one more club number (say, a 9 rather than an 8). If height is not desired, take one less club number (a 6 rather than a 7). It is better to be safe. On-course play often creates a bit of anxiety, which can counter your shot execution efforts. Play smart and allow for anxiety.

Trajectory control is also important when you are not in trouble. Consider the following situations. Which trajectory would be the most effective—normal, high, or low?

1. You are on the tee. The wind is to your back. There is no trouble in the fairway.
2. You are on the tee. The wind is in your face. There is no trouble in the fairway.
3. You are on the tee. There is a crosswind from right to left. There is no trouble in the fairway.
4. You are an 8-iron from the green with the wind to your back. The pin is back of center. There is no trouble in front.
5. You are an 8-iron from the green with the wind in your face. The pin is back of center. There is no trouble in front.

Low trajectory under the trees.

High trajectory over trees.

Figure 4.8. Apply trajectory control when going over or under trees.

6. You are a 6-iron from the green with the wind in your face. The pin is back of center. There is a sand trap around the front edge of the green.

7. You are a 6-iron from the green with the wind at your back. The pin is back of center. There is a sand trap around the front edge of the green.

These situations are regularly faced on the course. You may not have considered any shot other than your regular full-swing trajectory, which is fine if things are going well. If situations such as the ones presented have been causing you some wasted shots, however, think about the following alternatives. Remember that there is no "right" or "wrong" shot selection. Some shots are just more effective than others.

Situation Options

The first three situations involve determining the effects of the wind on your drive. A relatively high trajectory adds distance and is desirable in Situation 1. Therefore, if your normal full-swing trajectory is high, use it. However, that same high trajectory is less effective in Situations 2 and 3. If you tend to drive with a low trajectory, you may consider a 3-wood or a 4-wood off the tee in Situation 1 from your normal ball position.

If the wind is strong, the high shot loses considerable distance when hit into the wind. A high shot thrown into a crosswind could boomerang. A low shot usually penetrates the wind. Some distance will be lost, but control is gained, both into the wind and in the crosswind. A right-to-left crosswind adds roll to a right-to-left ball curvature and decreases the effects of a left-to-right curvature.

A normal low trajectory on your drives works to your advantage in Situations 2 and 3. If you tend to a low trajectory, you may consider a 3-wood or a 4-wood off the tee in Situation 1 from your normal ball position.

Situations 4-7 illustrate potential problems near the green. Approach shots to the green are often sent awry because more thought is not given to external effects. A good swing with the wrong club is not recommended when you are trying to make a number. The wind to your back tends to create overspin when a ball hits the green, and a ball travels farther in the air than normal.

In Situation 4, a low shot hit to the front of the green will roll to the back. There is less risk of losing control by throwing up a 9-iron into the wind. A controlled low shot will be less affected by the wind.

Situation 5 is an interesting shot with several options. Using one or two clubs more and making your regular swing compensates for the wind-reduced distance. Another choice is to hit a low shot with one or two more clubs, keeping the ball under the wind.

Situations 6 and 7 add one more variable to contend with, a sand trap. With these situations, the wind often becomes secondary to the trap and its possible consequences. Your objective now is to land on the green, and either the higher shot or your normal trajectory is desired. If you strike with descent, your normal shot may give you greater control when hitting the green. The higher shot has less spin control because the angle is more ascending at impact.

When possible, go with your normal shot. Be ready for situations that may require adaptations in your normal trajectory. The better your understanding of how to produce various shots, the more shots you have at your disposal, and in time, the better a player you will become.

SHORT GAME TECHNIQUES

The short game is often neglected, yet it is one of the most important phases of the game. All greens are not going to be hit in regulation by you or the pros. In a recent *Golf Digest* statistics section on male professionals, the leader in number of greens hit in regulation was Johnny Miller with .723 (72%). His scoring average was 71.34. This indicates that his short game must be pretty good. Another interesting statistic was Ray Floyd's scoring average, which was the lowest at 70.74. However, he was not listed in any statistics on sand saves, putting greens hit, driving accuracy, or distance. Therefore, he must also have a fine short game.

Up to this point, the advanced swing techniques have been primarily related to the full swing. Face, pace, and trajectory control, which were important in the full swing, are also important concepts in the short game.

The short game application presented in the basic swing techniques (Chapter 3) describing the mini-swings is used approximately 80% of the time in a round of golf. These techniques are the foundation for other more advanced concepts.

The present section, reprinted with permission of the National Golf Foundation (information sheet ES-14), is the work of Carol Johnson (1983), the Eastern consultant for the National Golf Foundation and former LPGA Teacher of the Year. She has developed a short game concept called "leveling." In this concept, the short game shots are presented by difficulty of the shots; as the shots require more variations in face, pace, and trajectory control, the level of difficulty increases.

When you find yourself 10-70 yards from the green, it is big decision time! Determining which club to use and which shot to hit often separates the champion from the "good" player.

Because there are many "approaches" to this part of the game of golf, there is also much confusion. In an effort to grade the more difficult shots, a "levels" approach has been created. It is designed to help you select the least complicated mechanical moves of the short swing. Often there is no need for complex or artificial methods to stop the ball when a simpler shot will do.

It is necessary to understand and be able to use a broad range of clubs for approach shots, ranging from the 4-iron through the sand wedge. Each club has distinct characteristics of loft, carry, and roll. The following list shows each club's personality:

Iron	Loft and Carry in Air	Roll
4	just under 1/3	2/3
5	1/3	2/3
6	just under 1/2	1/2
7	1/2	1/2
8	just under 2/3	1/3
9	2/3	1/3
Pitching Wedge	3/4	1/4
Sand Wedge	4/5	1/5

As you analyze the shot, the first question is where should the ball land? Once that question is answered, you simply choose the club that has the loft, carry, and roll to match the choice!

Now you must decide how to hit the ball. Again, the simplest way to perform the skill should be chosen. One simple way to swing a golf club and produce different results is to vary the length of the swing. Refer to the chart below to decide approximate matches between swing length and distance.

Swing Length	Approximate Distance
1-to-1	15-yard shot
2-to-2	30-yard shot
3-to-3	45-yard shot
4-to-4	60-yard shot

Knowing that each golfer will face a variety of situations in executing approach shots tends to make golf teachers skeptical of such a simplistic approach to the skills. However, these two charts provide the basis for all types of approach shots. What follows is a list of four progressive levels of types of shots, using these basic patterns.

Figure 4.9. Sequence shots of Level One demonstrate the one-level swing.

Level One

Requirements to perform the simplest short shot will have the following properties. Note how the properties vary with different distances (Figure 4.9).

1.
Distance: 15 yards.
Grip: Well down on the grip, close to the lower edge of the grip; medium grip pressure.
Aim: Clubface square to the target line.
Setup: Narrow stance (only 2-3 inches wide); square stance or very slightly open; 70% of weight on the target-side foot; little or no transfer of weight during the shot; resembles body posture for putting — imagine that you are putting with a lofted club.
Wrist action: Arms and shoulders form a triangle; entire triangle moves; little or no wrist action.

2.
Distance: 30 yards.
Grip: Halfway down on the grip; medium pressure.
Aim: Clubface square to the target line.
Setup: Narrow stance (4-5 inches wide); square stance or slightly open; weight equally distributed at address and transfers naturally with the shot; body posture and feel is still one of "sitting down" and smallness.
Wrist action: No noticeable wrist action; the triangle of the arms and shoulders remains firm throughout the shot.

3.
Distance: 45 yards.
Grip: Down on the grip 1 1/2-2 inches; medium grip pressure.
Aim: Clubface square to the target line.
Setup: Square stance or slightly open; weight equally distributed at address and transfers more noticeably with the shot; body posture's center of gravity as low as in previous shots.
Wrist action: At 3 on the backswing and at 3 on the forward swing, the wrists bend with a levering action to provide additional club and head speed and therefore more power.

On most golf courses, a golfer can play eighteen holes and use Level One shots for nearly 80% of all approach shots into the greens. Club selection will provide great variety to the loft, carry, and roll— needed for the various situations encountered.

Figure 4.10. Sequence shots of Level Two demonstrate a longer swing arc (4-to-4) with slower speed.

Level Two

For approach shots where conditions call for a shot that causes the ball to stop sooner than the normal loft, carry, and roll of a standard Level One shot, you must learn Level Two shots (Figure 4.10).

Imagine that you are 30 yards from the green. There is a sand bunker between the ball and the edge of the green. You must carry the ball 20 yards in the air, and there are 10 yards of roll to the flag. Depending upon the slope of the green, your 9-iron, pitching wedge, or sand wedge will carry the ball 2/3 distance in the air and allow 1/3 distance roll. Although the sand wedge shot rolls the least of the three choices, there are times during an approach situation when even he sand wedge shot will not stop soon enough. Having chosen to use the sand wedge, you must now change something about your swing to make the ball roll less than its normal 1/3 distance pattern.

The simplest change to make in the golf swing is in the speed of the swing. The 30-yard shot above would normally require a 2-to-2 swing length. But to stop the ball sooner, you will swing the club in a longer swing arc (4-to-4) while slowing down the speed of the swing, both backward and forward! When the ball is hit with this slower-but-longer swing, it will still travel the required distance in the air, but it will roll less when it lands. Learning to swing at different speeds is not easy. Practice is very important if you want to learn Level Two shots.

Level Two shots from any distance have the following properties.

Grip: Only slightly down on the grip; very light grip pressure.
Aim: Clubface is square to the target line.
Setup: Stance is slightly wider, more toward normal width for a swing; stance is square to the target line or very slightly open; weight is equally distributed and transfers naturally during the swing.
Speed: Very noticeably slow.

Even though it is very difficult to perform slower swings while maintaining swing rhythm, they should be mastered. In an average round of golf, approximately 10% of the approach shots will require this slower Level Two swing in order to produce shorter roll.

Figure 4.11. Sequence shots of Level Three demonstrate a combination of an open clubface with an outside-to-inside swing path.

Level Three

Level Three shots require even less roll than Level Two shots. Imagine again that you have a 30-yard shot with the sand bunker between the ball and the edge of the green. You must stop the ball even sooner to keep it from passing the hole. This requires even more swing adjustments, making the swing progressively more complex and difficult to master (Figure 4.11).

Level Three shots from any distance have the following properties.

Grip: Down on the grip 1-2 inches; medium grip pressure.

Aim: Clubface is open to the target; target-side foot is drawn back, making the stance definitely open to the target line; aim to the left of the target.

Setup: Normal stance width; stance definitely open to target to aid in change of swing path.

Path: Definite change from the normal path (inside-straight-inside) to an outside-inside path; weight transfers normally.

Speed: Brisk speed, more like Level One; a normal swing speed for the distance to be covered.

Length: A little longer than Level One for the same distance for a 30-yard Level One shot, the length would be about 2-to-2; for a 30-yard Level Three shot, the length would be 3-to-3 .

On a shot with the clubface open and using a normal swing path, the ball would slice to the right. A square clubface on an outside-to-inside swing path would produce a ball that goes straight to the left of target. Level Three shots combine the open face with the outside-to-inside swing path to produce a cut shot that stops the ball much sooner than necessary for all but 5% of the approach shots in a typical round of eighteen holes.

Figure 4.12. Sequence shots of Level Four demonstrate changes in speed, path, face, and angle of approach.

Level Four

Level Four shots require the least amount of roll of any approach shot. These are the shots that must stop when hitting the downhill slope of a green, for example. Instead of having the 10, or even 5, yards of roll that were allowed in the Level Two and Level Three shots from 30 yards, a Level Four shot must have a "super stop!" To do this, you must change four areas — speed, path, face, and angle of approach. A Level Four shot would have the following properties (Figure 4.12).

Grip: Almost at the top of the grip, as in a full shot; light grip pressure.
Aim: Clubface open to the target line; target-side foot and shoulder open to the target line.
Setup: Normal stance width, definitely open stance, shoulders also open; ball position is slightly further back in the stance than normal; weight will transfer as in a normal shot.
Path: Outside to inside, much more than normal; the path follows the opened stance footline.
Speed: Very slow and sustained.
Length: Longer than normal (for a 30-yard shot, 4-to-4).
Angle of Approach: Sharper and more descending on the forward swing because the club is taken outside the target line on the backswing.
Impact: The heel of the club passes through the impact area well ahead of the toe of the club because the clubface is open to the line.

This level of shot can be used from the grass or as an explosion shot from a sand bunker. It is the most difficult shot to master and is seldom used. Less than 5% of all approach shots during a round will require this type of shot.

If you want to perfect all four levels of approach shots, you will need organized practice situations in which you use the various clubs from 4-iron through sand wedge from the same location to the same target. This will teach the basic loft, carry, and roll of each club. The second stage of learning is to practice each club from different distances, each club at 15 yards, each at 30 yards, each at 45 yards, and each at 60 yards. And, finally, you must practice each level to be able to manipulate the amount of green and the terrain of the green. As you learn the mechanics of the four levels, the approach shots in golf become more manageable and the improvement in scoring becomes more noticeable. A summary of the approach shot levels is provided in Table 4.2.

Table 4.2
Summary of the Approach-Shot Levels

	Level One	Level Two	Level Three	Level Four
Percentage of Shots	80%	10%	5%	5%
Club Selection	5-9 iron, pitching wedge or sand wedge	pitching wedge or sand wedge	pitching wedge or sand wedge	pitching wedge or sand wedge
Speed	lively	very slow and sustained	lively	very slow and sustained
Path	target line	target line	left	left
Face	square to target	square to target	open	open
Angle of Approach	upswing	upswing	upswing	upswing
Grip	standard	standard with lighter grip pressure	standard	standard with lighter grip pressure
Aim	square shoulders; slightly open feet and hips	standard	open (all)	open (all)
Setup	feet fairly close; ball position forward; weight favors target foot	feet wider than Level One; ball position forward; weight even on both feet	feet fairly close; ball position forward; weight favors target foot	feet fairly close; ball position forward; weight favors target foot

118

Width of Arc	grip club within 2-3" from the top	grip club 1-2" from the top	same as Level Two	grip club 2" from top
Hand position	standard	standard	standard with open clubface	standard with open clubface
Length of Arc	2-to-2	4-to-4	3-to-3	4/5 to 4/5
Lever	one	two	same as Level Two	same as Level Two
Timing	standard	standard	standard	standard
Plane	standard	standard	upright	upright
Release	none	yes	yes	yes
Fixed Center	slightly in front of ball at address and maintained	even with ball	even with ball	even with ball
Balance	weight transfers as a reaction to the shot	weight transfers	weight transfers	weight transfers, resembles full shot
Skill Level Necessary	beginner to advanced	intermediate to advanced	advanced	advanced

Summary

The advanced techniques that have been presented are fun to practice and rewarding to execute during play. These techniques are developed through a solid foundation in basic fundamentals. Remember: No player is ever too advanced to stop checking and rechecking the basics: grip, setup position, and alignment.

5

CHALLENGE SHOTS

Challenge shots are what the name implies. They "challenge" you to deviate from your normal, secure swing. Challenge shots require adaptations in your setup position to accommodate the situation. Because of the less familiar setup position, they often cause a break in your routine. They test your composure and shot execution creativity. Do you panic with a ball below your feet on a 40 degree downslope, or do you remain calm and plan the shot? If your ball lands under a low-hanging tree branch 10 yards from the green, do you take an unplayable lie or knock it out from under the tree onto the green?

This section will provide technique and understanding for playing the challenging shots. Uneven lies, backward shots, and under-tree knee shots will be discussed.

UNEVEN LIES

Uneven lies are situations in which your feet and the ball are not on the same level. When this occurs, changes in the normal setup position are necessary to accommodate the effects of the slope angle on posture, balance, ball contact, and curvature. The severity of the slope dictates the modifications in the setup. This, in turn, may influence the potential swing pace and swing length. The following guidelines will assist you in establishing the setup position for uneven lies:

- Make practice swings away from the ball, but on the same slope angle as the one on which the ball is positioned.
- Note the effects of the slope on your posture, balance, and low point of your swing.
- Establish a swing pace and swing length you can control relative to the slope angle.

Based on your individual swing tendencies, your practice swings will help you identify the necessary setup position. Your sense of balance relative to the slope angle will help determine the weight distribution at address (back, center, or forward on your feet, or more to the target or rear side). Your swing balance (or lack of balance) will help establish the potential swing length and swing pace you will be able to control, as well as the dictated ball position. Your posture will be affected more on sidehill lies, in which the ball is either above or below your feet, because the ball is closer to or farther away from you, depending upon the angle of the slope.

A summary chart of uneven lies is provided in Table 5.1. It is important to understand the similarities and differences. It will be helpful to group uneven lies as uphill and downhill lies and as sidehill lies. Allow common sense to be your guide. The severity of the slope will provide you with direction. The less even the slope, the less the setup and results will differ from "normal." As the slope becomes more severe, swing balance is a major concern. This affects the swing length and pace. Use your best judgment. It is better to get back into position for the next shot than to play for a miracle and get deeper into trouble.

Table 5.1
Summary Chart for Uneven Lies

	Uphill or Downhill	Sidehill Ball Above	Sidehill Ball Below
Setup	Weight is more toward the high foot	Weight into hill, midstep to balls of feet	Weight into hill, midstep to heels
	Lean into hill	Slightly taller posture	Maintain posture over ball
	Ball position toward the high foot	Choke down on club	Use one more for extra length, 3/4 swing
	Set shoulders parallel to the contour of the land	Ball position slightly to target side of center	Ball position target side of center
Curvature	Uphill lies tend to draw	Tend to hook or draw	Tend to fade or slice
	Downhill lies tend to fade	Aim slightly right of target	Aim slightly center of target
Distance	Uphill adds loft to shot (one more club)	Same to more distance	Same to less distance
	Downhill decreases loft (one less club)		

Practice Application

Whenever possible, practice the uneven lies. Practice provides you with an opportunity to experience the modifications in your setup position and swing balance. Often, the initial contrast in feel is a greater intimidation and cause for mishits than the actual shot execution.

Practice ranges usually do not have areas designated for practicing uneven lies. However, most ranges do have elevated tees. The banks of the tee area will at least provide you with an opportunity to simulate the uneven lies. It would be helpful to buy some plastic golf balls to use for practicing these lies. They are inexpensive and safe. Practice swings in the various lies are fine, however, actually swinging at the plastic balls is better.

The following practice suggestions will provide you with a means to compare your normal setup position and swing feel with that dictated by the slope angle. The objective is to become more aware of the differences in the setup position when hitting from uneven lies. Each one of the four types of uneven lies is illustrated in the setup position (Figures 5.1 to 5.4). The exercises and drills should be practiced with each of the uneven lies.

**Figure 5.1. Setup position —
uphill lie.**

**Figure 5.2. Setup position —
downhill lie.**

123

Figure 5.3. Setup position — sidehill lie, ball above feet.

Figure 5.4. Setup position — sidehill lie, ball below the feet.

Drills

Note:Use back bank of elevated tee. Place two clubs on a slope. One club is placed vertical to the slope, the other is horizontal. The clubs provide a reference for ball position and stance.

1. Take your normal setup. Make practice swings. Note the following:
  • Where is the low point of your arc?
  • How does your posture feel?
  • How is your balance at address? During the swing? At the finish?
  • How is your swing pace? Length?

2. Hit four plastic balls from your normal setup.
  • What are the results?

3. Modify your setup to the slope angle, using the suggested guidelines provided in Table 5.1, and make practice swings.
- Where is the low point of your arc? Same? Toward the high foot? Toward the low foot?
- How does your posture feel? Same? Closer? Farther?
- How is your balance? At address? During the swing? At the finish?
- How is your swing pace? Length?

4. Hit four plastic balls in your modified setup.
- What are the results?

5. Take your normal setup position and make practice swings.
- Note the differences in feel at the address, during the swing, and at the finish.

Practice uneven lies, using the full swing and mini-swings with extreme and very slight slopes in the practice procedures presented. Your ability to feel the differences and to make the indicated modifications can be a deciding factor in your scores on courses with varying terrain, particularly if your home course is relatively flat.

Course Application

Uneven lies are almost always prevalent around greens and hazards. Because the swings around the green are shorter and have less motion, balance is less critical. However, the slope will influence ball trajectory, distance, and curvature. Setup position remains very important to achieve the desired results. The suggested guidelines in Table 5.1 should be followed with the shorter swings.

The following situations around the greens are common. Often a particular decision is made and a club is chosen for a shot and later regretted, because your body tension was not considered.

Situations

1. You are 15 feet off the green on a slight uphill slope. You have mini-swing (one-lever) to a pin on the back part of an elevated green.

Considerations
- Loft is added to the club by the slope.
- Loft increases air time and decreases roll.
- Compensating for loss of distance due to loft requires a longer swing.
- The longer the swing, the less the control.
- Loft reduces percentages for accurate placement.
- Loft into an uphill slope decreases roll.

Club choice: 6- or 7-iron.

125

2. You are 15 feet off the green on a severe downhill slope of thick grass. You have a mini-swing (one-lever) to a pin on the front of a flat green.

Considerations:
- Loft is reduced on the club by the slope.
- Less loft increases roll and decreases air time.
- Less loft requires a shorter swing.
- More control with shorter swing.
- Land on the green.

Club Choice: Pitching a wedge or sand wedge.

3. You are in the back part of a bunker, close to the edge on a down slope toward the green. The bunker is 15 feet wide with a 5-foot-high overhanging lip on the green side. The pin is 30 feet from the trap.

Considerations:
- Balance!
- Must create a stance.
- Penalty for grounding your club on the backswing.
- Potential for burying the ball in the lip.
- Slope takes loft off the sand wedge.

Club Choice: Sand wedge and retreat.(Find the highest percentage exit out of the sand.)

Terrain influences ball trajectory. Consequently, when playing shots around the green, the terrain often dictates the type of shot selected. For example, think about playing a pitch shot over a trap to a tight pin placement. If your lie is flat or slightly uphill, this is a fairly easy shot because of the high trajectory usually obtained. However, if the ball is on a downhill slope with the same conditions, the usually high trajectory with little roll is altered to a lower and flatter trajectory with increased roll. Visions of getting the ball close may need to change to visions of getting the ball on the green safely.

Fairway shots must also be altered because of the severity of the slope. For example, the distance factor may dictate a wood, but the slope dictates a higher percentage with an iron. There are no right or wrong decisions. Experience is a great teacher. With practice, you will begin to know your capabilities in playing uneven lies. The more exposure you have to playing uneven lies, the more comfortable you will become. You will begin to think less and allow your body to respond more naturally to the situation.

BACKWARD SHOTS

Is it hard to imagine backward shots? Probably, because they are rarely seen. Yet they are useful to know and can save strokes.

There are two backward shots. You can reverse the club and swing in the opposite direction (a right-handed player swings left-handed), or you can turn your back to the target and swing. Surprisingly, the backward shots are quite easy and fun to execute.

Backward shots are most commonly used in situations when the choice is either to get the ball back into play or to take an unplayable lie. The situation depicted in Figure 5.5 is quite common. For many, this is an immediately unplayable lie. However, with some practice, the backward shot can turn this stroke loss into a stroke saver and distance gain.

Figure 5.5. On-course application of the "true" backward shot.

127

The backward shots should be practiced, as should all shots, prior to their use on the course. There are two fundamental shots: the switch hit and the back to target. You will probably feel more comfortable with one or the other shot. For example, if you have played baseball or softball, reversing the club can be compared to switch hitting; it is the same motion in the opposite direction. If you have played polo, the back-to-target shot is similar to the backward pass.

To practice the switch-hit, reversed-club shot, you take the opposite grip position. Your target hand becomes the low hand and your rear hand becomes the high hand. Use your interlock or overlap grip. Note the difference in the clubhead position illustrated in Figure 5.6. A more lofted club provides a larger hitting surface. If you have a putter, such as a bull's eye putter in which both sides are flat, it is a good club for this shot. The shot will produce an extremely low trajectory, almost a total roll, but can be effective for getting back into play.

Figure 5.6. Setup position for the backward shot, using the reverse side of the clubhead.

Address.   Backswing.

Follow-through.

Figure 5.7. Sequence shots of the "true" backward shot.

As you practice hitting balls on the range, you will develop a feel for how much control you can obtain. Initially practice with mini-swings. As you gain confidence, you may want to expand the swing length. Rhythm is important. Think of a pendulum swing that is even on both sides. Power and distance are not critical. Your sole objective is to get the ball out of trouble and back into play.

The true backward shot (back to target) has the greatest potential for distance and direction of the two shots. Figure 5.7 illustrates the setup position and the upward and downward motion. Note the clubhead position and the corresponding grip in the setup in the first picture of the sequence. The clubface is toward the target. The rear arm is hanging freely, with the palm of the hand facing the target. The club is held near the bottom of the grip. The ball is positioned somewhere between your ankle and just forward of your toes, in line with the clubhead. Practice swings will help you determine the low point of the swing arc, which determines your ball position.

The club is an extension of your arm, as may be seen in the sequence of pictures. Your arm and club work as a unit, with no wrist action. This is a one-lever motion up and down.

From the setup position, the upward motion is made by extending your arm and club together to the desired swing height as illustrated in the backswing in the sequence. As you swing down, your upper body bends forward to provide additional support for the arm swing (last picture in the sequence). This is important because the shoulder joint has a limited backward range of motion.

Practice this shot with various swing lengths and speed. Start short and slow and use a medium to lofted club. This shot can be mastered quickly because of the one-lever motion.

Course Application

When considering using the backward shots, remember that you need space to swing and a good lie. The amount of space necessary will be determined as you practice. You will become aware of the minimal and maximal swing length that you can control. If there is any doubt whether you can execute the shot in a given situation and the score is the important goal for your round, take an unplayable lie.

When you are out playing and practicing various shots on the course, practice the backward shots to develop a better feel. Put the ball next to trees in the woods and areas around the green. Try both, but only after practicing on the range first.

UNDER-TREE SHOT

This shot is another stroke saver. It is not a shot that is needed often, but it is good to know the shot, just in case.

When your ball goes under a tree, it is often possible to make a swing, but the normal swing arc may be too long or high. By making a few modifications in your stance and swing plane, you can save a shot and gain good position and distance rather than take an unplayable lie.

Two variations of the under-tree shots will be presented here. The two address positions are illustrated in Figure 5.8 and Figure 5.9. By lowering your body, as demonstrated in both shots, your swing plane becomes flatter and your swing arc lower. Your swing resembles a baseball swing in that it tends to be more horizontal than vertical.

Figure 5.8. Setup position for the under-the-tree shot, "letting the air out of your tires."

Lower-body motion is restricted, as can be noted in the setup positions for both shots. The leg positions allow the height reduction in the shots. These shots are played primarily with arm and hand motion. The club is gripped closer to the shaft and the swing length is 3/4 for greater control.

The shot illustrated in Figure 5.8 is often described as "letting the air out of your tires." The stance is widened, with the knees flexed in. The arms are extended, which allows the motion of the swing to be more around the body, in a flatter plane.

The knee shot allows for the maximal lowering of the body. Notice in Figure 5.9 how the back is tilted slightly forward to allow the arms some freedom from the body. This shot requires greater arm control because of the shallowness of the club angle on the forward swing. There is less room for error.

The woods are good clubs for the under-tree shots. They provide the greatest hitting space and the least loft.

In determining the potential of your shot selection, consider the lie. Both under-tree shots produce a relatively shallow angle of approach because of the flatter arc. More descent is possible with the wider base than with the knee shot because there is more potential height

Figure 5.9. Setup position for the under-the-tree knee shot.

variation. If the ball is on the surface of the ground, or if it has a good lie, then both could be used. As the lie becomes marginal, the knee shot becomes less desirable. Remember that the purpose of the shots is to save strokes.

It is beneficial to practice both shots on the practice tee and then in the actual situation. The following suggestions for your practice sessions encourage experimentation in different situations. These will help you identify possibilities when the shots are realistic and unrealistic to attempt.

Practice Suggestions
- Hit from good and bad lies.
- Have a friend hold a club to simulate a tree (Figure 5.10).
- Use woods and irons.
- Vary the height of your body with the wide stance.

Figure 5.10. Practice with a friend who is simulating the tree.

133

As you practice, note the difference in trajectory and roll produced in different situations. Which shots and situations have the greatest potential for execution? Which combinations are your most comfortable? Most uncomfortable?

Summary

Challenge shots are fun to practice and to share with your friends. They are good shots to have in your bag. Though they may rarely be used, you will be prepared to save strokes when the time comes.

6

PRACTICE STRATEGIES

Practice makes playing fun. It provides you with an opportunity to develop mechanically sound technique, feel for your swing execution, confidence in your swing, and mental composure. These opportunities, through practice, will ultimately enhance your ability to execute and score on the course.

Practice, to many people, is "beating golf balls." They relate the number of balls struck to the quality of practice. Unfortunately, there is not a one-to-one correspondence between the number of balls struck and the amount of golf improvement achieved. People strike golf balls for many reasons, including recreation, exercise, thinking time, therapy for stress release, and swing improvement. The only common denominator of these reasons is the actual striking of the golf ball. An improved golf swing and subsequent play improvement are not necessarily outcomes of just striking balls. Practice through striking balls and playing must be directed toward some method or purpose to be effective in improving your swing and playing ability.

As you begin to get excited about golf, or if you are already highly motivated to improve, you must determine what your objectives are for practicing. Ask yourself the following questions:

- How much mental and physical effort do I want to expend for improvement? Low? Medium? High?
- How much do I want to improve? A little? A lot?
- How much time do I want to commit to practice? Once a week? Twice a week? Three times a week? More than three times a week?
- Why do I want to improve?

There are no right or wrong answers to these questions. They do, however, help you establish a mind-set for practice. Your mind-set is important. The rate and status of your golf improvement is determined by the effectiveness of your practice sessions. The quality, not just the quantity of practice sessions, is critical.

135

Practice should be and can be fun. People often equate practices of any sort with work rather than fun. True, improvement requires effort to be expended, both mentally and physically, and the road to improvement is not always a smooth one. There can be many frustrations along the way, but there can still be joy in the effort.

This chapter will provide you with an understanding of "how to practice." Organizing your practice sessions will help you make the most effective use of your time and energy. Time, in terms of minutes and hours, is not the critical element in practice efficiency. The structure of your efforts, related to mental and physical execution, is important. For example, when practicing, if you are trying to perfect the hand position at the top, are you concentrating on the feet of the position or are you concerned with the ball going to the target? Or, if you are trying to hit a designated target, are you thinking about the mechanics of the shot or the target? These two questions may seem to be saying the same thing. However, when practicing, the emphasis is quite different and the two corresponding thoughts are incompatible.

This chapter will discuss when you should think about and work on mechanical aspects of your swing and when you should think about the ball going to the target. Additional information is provided to help you learn from the ball flight how your swing works in a cause-and-effect relationship. Visual aids and drills that will enhance your practice sessions are suggested.

HOW TO PRACTICE

Your practice strategies and practice needs should reflect your own style and skill level. Your practice may be specific, such as for your short game, or general, in which both the full and short game are stressed. Some days you may practice a short time and other days you may practice longer. You may practice alone, with a friend, or in a group, such as a team. In time, you will become aware of how you practice most effectively. The following four questions may help you establish a practice guide.

- When do I practice most effectively? Morning? Afternoon? Evening?
- Where do I practice most effectively? Corner of the range? Middle of the range? Park?
- Who do I practice with most effectively? One other? Several others? No one?
- What do I practice? Mechanics? Target? Feel? Play?

When

This is often dictated by your previous commitments to work, family, or school. Practice may have to be scheduled according to free time. For example, if you are a morning person and your schedule only permits late-afternoon practice, you can learn to be effective in the afternoon. Or if you have a family with children to work around, your schedule may fluctuate. However, your practice time can still be effective. There are drills that you can do in your backyard or in a park. Even just thirty minutes of concentrated practice at a range is better than six hours playing on the course.

Where

In your initial stages of learning and becoming comfortable with yourself as a golfer, you may find that less populated areas on the range are best for your practice sessions. Often, if you have practice balls of your own, parks or fields are good places to practice. As you become more comfortable, it will be beneficial to practice where other people are around. It will develop your concentration and prepare you for such actual situations as the first tee on a Saturday morning.

If you are more highly skilled, the place of practice becomes less intimidating. Your attention is more focused. However, if you are bothered by people seeking your advice on their games, you may want to find a more secluded area.

Who

The person or persons with whom you practice is a preference related to your needs. As you begin to play golf, it is often beneficial to find another interested friend who enjoys practicing and playing. Each of you can motivate the other. You can share in the learning process and help each other. Having an external motivator such as a friend helps you establish a routine or habit of practicing and playing.

As your skill progresses, you may find that you practice best alone. You may become internally motivated to practice. This is not to say that you necessarily isolate yourself from others while practicing. It only implies that you develop adequate self-direction without the reinforcement of others.

What

The when, where, and who provide the external structure to your practice routine. The what of practice is the foundation for improvement. What do you think about when practicing—mechanics, feel, target? What can you use to enhance your practice? And, what do you learn from practicing?

137

PRACTICE THOUGHTS

Practice thoughts are divided into two orientations: Process and product. Process orientation emphasizes feel and the development of technique. Product orientation emphasizes the result of the swing technique, such as ball flight. Both of these orientations are important in practice. They are, however, generally incompatible when thought of simultaneously within one swing motion.

Process Orientation

In a practice session, process orientation relates to developing your swing technique through body awareness. You must try to match the kinesthetic feel of the swing motion with the desired technique relative to specific swing check points. For example, if you are working on the mini-swing, 3-to-3 swing length, you may be trying to feel the timing of the wrist action in the cocking-uncocking-cocking of the wrist through the ball. A drill using a tee in the grip end of the club helps identify the swing check points. The tee points to the ground on the backswing (3) and on the follow-through (3) with the desired wrist action. Wrist action that is too early or too late results in the tee pointing in a direction other than the ground.

When you are working on the "feel" of the swing, the actual results of the swing (indicated by ball flight) are only secondarily important. The feel of the specific motion or part of the motion is the primary focus. The following is an example of a process-oriented swing motion. Assume that your basic fundamentals of setup are in order:

Target
An area 50 yards away. Use clubs as directional guides for alignment and setup.
Goal
To feel the wrist action involved in executing the 3-to-3 mini-swing.
Swing Intent
Using the tee-down drill, to point the tee to the ground on the backward and forward swings and identify the feel.
Swing Result
The swing check points and the associated feeling of motion were identified.

Anytime that you practice, whether process or product thought is emphasized, you should direct your swing motion toward a specific target. Directional clubs placed on the ground provide a good reference for motion as well as establishing your setup position and body awareness toward a target.

The goal for the swing motion in this example is to feel the wrist action in the 3-to-3 mini-swing. Your thoughts are directed to an internal awareness of your wrist action. For example, if you tend to be stiff in your hands and wrist, you may want to hold the club very lightly in your hands, allowing your wrist to be more active. The contrasting feel will be loose instead of stiff.

To accomplish your goal, the tee-down drill provides you with check points. The 3-to-3 mini-swing has your hands and arms at hip level with the angle of the club pointing up. The tee in the grip end of the club is pointed toward the ground.

The result of your swing motion relates to the associated feeling in your hands and wrist when matched with the swing check points provided by the drill. For example, with a reduced-tension grip you may feel more freedom in the swing motion than with a stiff wrist. You may also feel more clubhead speed, which you had not felt before. Your thoughts are internal and relate to body awareness relative to the desired swing techniques.

During practice, regardless of your skill level, the feel of a specific motion or attaining a particular position in your swing is often initially achieved best without using a ball (practice swings). This helps focus your attention on swing thoughts or internal feelings. The consequences of striking the ball does not interfere with your kinesthetic awareness. You should try to make enough practice swings to recognize the desired feel prior to hitting a ball. As you proceed to hit practice balls, continue to relate the feelings you established in your practice swing, regardless of the initial ball results. As you continue to practice, the desired results will occur.

If you are just beginning to play golf, your technique and swing motion may be erratic when you practice. In time, you will become more consistent. Initially, allow your developing technique to establish some consistency to your ball flight. Once a pattern is established and your swing is more consistent, you can compare feel with the ball flight characteristics you like.

When you are concentrating on a specific phase of the swing motion, your attention is focused on the feel of the swing or body position at that phase. This may temporarily interfere with the timing or flow of the whole swing motion and may affect the desired results. Remember: The feel of a swing motion, or making the desired motion technically efficient, is the most important objective during the process-orientation phase of practice.

Product Orientation

The resulting ball flight is the product of your swing motion. For many of you, this may seem to be the primary purpose of practice. Ultimately, when you are playing on the course, the prime concern is the result. Initially, however, you must develop a swing motion that is mechanically efficient and creates a kinesthetic awareness of the desired motion. This allows you to produce the desired ball flight.

During the product orientation of practice, you are trying to match the intent of the swing motion (desired ball flight) with the outcome of the swing motion (resulting ball flight). The following example of a product-oriented swing motion is provided as a contrast to the process-oriented swing motion previously presented. The 3-to-3 mini-swing is the intended shot. Let's assume that your basic fundamentals of setup are in order:

Target
A circle with a 10-yard radius, 50 yards away.
Goal
To land the ball within the circle.
Swing Intent (Desired Ball Flight)
Using the 3-to-3 mini-swing, ball flight should start on target with a high trajectory and land in the target areas.
Swing Result (Resulting Ball Flight)
Ball flight started on target with a high trajectory and landed in the target area.

The target in the product-oriented phase is more specific. The goal is external and relates to the swing outcome. It is specific in that it defines the direction, landing area, distance the ball must travel in the air, and the designated size of the landing area. The swing intent is specific to the results. The swing feel is preprogrammed through practice swings. The following swing characteristics are matched with the desired ball flight characteristics in order to produce the intended swing:

- Setup position (ball position, alignment, posture);
- Swing length (3-to-3);
- Swing pace (swing speed) necessary to send the ball 50 yards in in the air;
- Angle of approach necessary to create a high trajectory.

The swing result is matched with the swing intent. Did you accomplish what you intended to do? Did the ball reach the target with the desired ball flight?

LEARNING FROM BALL FLIGHT

Ball flight provides you with immediate feedback on your swing motion. It helps you answer the question "Why?"—"Why did I accomplish my swing intent?" and "Why did I not accomplish my swing intent?"

Swing Intent Matches Result

A match between intent and results is reinforcing. It provides you with positive feedback that your efforts are bringing results. You are beginning to accomplish your goals in developing technique and feel.

After each swing match, take time to allow the feeling of the swing motion and associated information of ball flight to make an impression. Review the swing; it only takes a few seconds:

- My swing intent was . . .
- My setup was . . .
- My swing pace was . . .
- My swing length was . . .
- My angle of approach was . . .
- My swing result was . . .

Each swing becomes part of a data file. The more swing matches that are stored with corresponding associated information, the greater potential you have for reproducing those results.

Mismatch of Swing Intent and Result

As much can be learned from a mismatch between intent and result as from a match. Many golfers lack the understanding to cope with a mismatch. A mismatch to them is an indication of "failure." They try to cover their "failure" by hitting another ball as fast as they can. This is not a good strategy because it eventually compounds the error.

After a mismatch, take time to determine the cause. What was the ball flight? Review your swing with the same approach as with your swing match:

- My swing intent was . . .
- My setup was . . .
- My swing pace was . . .
- My swing length was . . .
- My angle of approach was . . .
- My swing result was . . .

By rationally approaching your swing mismatches with the self-questioning swing review, you can find the cause of your mismatched ball flight.

Interpreting Ball Flight

You gain the greatest benefit from ball flight information as you become more consistent in your swing technique and develop a swing timing and tempo. As this occurs, your ball flight becomes more consistent. Regardless of the ball flight characteristics, it is more predictable, as are the swing techniques causing the ball flight.

What consistency in swing direction and distance should you seek? No one achieves 100% consistency because we are human, not machines. Nonetheless, we strive for perfection — to do so is within the nature of the game's challenge. Realistically, if you are just beginning, 5% would be excellent. If you are advanced, 80% or better is desirable.

The important key to interpreting ball flight is to first have some consistent pattern. Initially, the pattern may not be what you ultimately desire in your ball-flight characteristics. However, it will provide you with some basis for comparison.

Ball flight has two basic components—direction and distance. These are affected by the ball flight influences presented in Chapter 2. The components and the influences are indicated for reference in Table 6.1. Your ability to interpret your ball flight and to self-correct depends on your understanding of the ball influences and their effect on distance and direction, and of the corresponding swing relationship.

Table 6.1

Ball Flight Components and Ball Flight Influences Affecting Them

Direction:
- Path
- Face
- Squareness of Contact

Distance:
- Speed
- Angle of Approach
- Face
- Squareness of Contact

Each ball flight influence has three alternatives—two extremes and a middle point, which we will say theoretically is our desired option (Table 6.2).

Table 6.2
Ball Flight Influences and their Options

Influences	Extreme	Options Desired	Extreme
Speed	fast	medium	slow
Path	left	straight	right
Face	closed	square	open
Angle of Approach	steep	descent/ascent	shallow
Squareness of Contact	heel	centroid	toe

You have control over each of these in your swing. Obviously, as your skill improves, you will obtain greater control, which will allow you to execute the advanced swing techniques presented in Chapter 4. But regardless of your skill level, you can understand how each of these influences ball flight and the things that affect each in your swing.

Speed

Distance is affected by speed. You have or will develop a swing speed that you can control and repeat. Many golfers try to obtain a normal swing speed that is 85% of maximum controllable speed. This provides a reserve for a little extra distance when needed (or a little less) and it is repeatable. Your distance range for each club is more easily determined. You control swing speed by having three gears—fast, medium (your normal), and slow. This, in turn, allows you to control the distance the ball goes.

Path

Direction is determined by the path of club at impact. Your arms and shoulders control the swing path. Let's assume that your setup and alignment are on target. When you swing, if your arms are swinging to the right of target at impact (inside-out path), the ball will start to the right of target. Conversely, if at impact your arms are swinging to the left of target (outside-in path), the ball will start left of target. A straight path or on-target path results when your arms are swinging down the target line at impact. Your arms tend to follow your shoulder line. You can control the path by becoming more aware of the influence of your arms and shoulders.

Face

The clubface position at impact imparts spin to the ball. This affects both direction and distance. As the ball slows down, the resulting spin determines the curvature. The degree of openness or closedness dictates the amount of spin.

For the right-handed golfer, an open face imparts a clockwise spin, which results in a degree of curvature from a slight fade to a slice, or "banana ball." The counterclockwise spin of a closed face produces a degree of curvature from a slight draw to a hook, or "duck hook." The square clubface at impact produces an end-over-end spin and a relatively straight ball.

Your hands control the face of the club at impact. You can influence the ball flight curvature by increasng or decreasing your hand action, which produces a draw to a hooking action or a fade to a slice, respectively.

You can also influence the ball flight curvature through your grip position and grip pressure. A grip position in which your target hand is on top of the club, the rear hand is more under, and the grip pressure is light tends to increase the hand action (e.g., a draw becomes a hook). The opposite grip position (the target hand more under the club, the rear hand on top of the club, and a tight grip pressure) tends to decrease the hand action (e.g., a fade becomes a slice). You can control the clubface and therefore the curvature.

Angle of Approach

The angle at which the club contacts the ball determines the trajectory and affects the distance that the ball will travel. The ball position in your stance influences the angle of approach; the farther back toward your rear foot the ball is positioned in your stance, the lower the trajectory. Conversely as you move the ball forward in your stance toward your target foot, the trajectory is higher. For example, if you play your 7-iron in the middle of your stance, you obtain an average trajectory for your swing motion. As you move the ball toward your rear foot, with no other swing changes, loft is taken off the club. This produces a lower trajectory with a more descending angle of approach. If the ball is moved forward in the stance, it will increase the loft of the club and produce a higher trajectory than the normal (or middle ball) position. The angle of approach is more ascending. Therefore, you can control the angle of approach by altering the ball position in your stance.

Squareness of Contact

This is the hardest to control in the full swing when you are beginning to play golf. There is such a small difference between a square hit and an off-center hit, yet the off-center hit affects both the distance and direction. At first, just concentrate on the club contacting the ball somewhere. You will have greatest control of squareness of contact in your short game strokes because the potential margin for error is increased as the length of swing and swing motion decrease. As your timing and swing-motion improve, your ball contact will become more solid.

Table 6.2 illustrates the many possible ball flights that can be produced. You can produce various combinations at will or alter them singularly. Practice changing your ball flight by playing in the extremes. The following practice suggestions provide you with an opportunity to experiment with producing various ball flights. By practicing in the extremes, you can more readily identify the cause and effect relation between swing motion and ball flight. This allows you to understand the "why?" of the ball flight you produce by your swing—in practice and during play. You can begin to understand "why" you hit the ball to the left of target when you were lined up on target, or "why" you hit the ball fat instead of your usual crisp shot, or "why" you sliced the ball instead of hitting your usual draw. Practice and play become more fun because you are in control.

Practice Suggestions

The following practice drills will help you understand and learn to control your ball flight. Take your setup position toward a target. Use a club of your choice.

Speed
- Hit five balls at your normal swing speed.
- Hit five balls, increasing your swing speed.
- Hit five balls, decreasing your swing speed.
- Hit five balls at your normal swing speed.

Note the differences in the distance the ball goes when the speed is varied.

Path
Do not alter your setup position from the target.
- Hit five balls on path to your target.
- Hit five balls right of target.
- Hit five balls left of target.
- Hit five balls on path to your target.

How did you change your path? Can you feel and see the difference in your path when your shoulders are overactive or when your arms are more in control?

Face
Do these drills first by increasing or decreasing your grip pressure. Repeat by altering your grip position.
- Hit five balls with your normal curvature.
- Hit five balls, hooking.
- Hit five balls, slicing.
- Hit five balls with your normal curvature.

Which method is easier for you to control — the curvature, grip pressure, or grip position? Can you feel the difference in clubhead control and see the resulting effects by increasing or decreasing your hand action?

Angle of Approach
- Hit five balls from your normal ball position.
- Hit five balls from a back ball position.
- Hit five balls from a forward ball position.
- Hit five balls from your regular position.

What are the results in trajectory by altering ball position? What are the effects on distance?

145

Squareness of Contact

Use a putter at a distance of 20 feet from a hole, relatively flat if possible. Try to maintain the same swing speed and swing length on a square path.

- Hit five balls on the sweet spot.
- Hit five balls on the toe.
- Hit five balls on the heel.

What were the differences in distance? What were the differences in direction?

IMPORTANCE OF DRILLS IN PRACTICE

Practice drills can make your sessions on the tee more effective and motivating. Combining with the use of practice aids, they provide immediate visual and kinesthetic feedback. They help you compare what is felt in your swing with what is actually happening.

In developing your swing, it is impossible to concentrate on all aspects of motion at one time. It is important to have a basic feel for the whole swing motion as discussed in previous chapters. Once this feeling is established, specific aspects of the swing can be practiced by using drills. The drills are designed to develop feel and technique in different areas (path, face, pace, target-side awareness, etc.). For example, the arm and hand action can be isolated from the body motion. A drill in which the lower body is still and only the arms and hands are moving is used to emphasize the desired motion. This makes it easier for you to focus on the feel and technique without trying to remember or worry about everything else.

Drills are an important part of practice. The following guidelines are suggestions for effective use of drills in the development of your swing technique and feel.

Guidelines for Drill Effectiveness:

- Overuse promotes abuse
- Variety adds spice
- Consider safety
- Accept the challenge

Correct Use

The drill should be used correctly if it is to be effective. For example, you may be working on a drill to help you feel your posture through impact. If, as you are implementing the drill, you are raising up or standing erect initially, then the effectiveness of the drill is lost. Know the purpose for which you are using a drill and concentrate on that aspect.

Learning from Ball Flight

Ball flight feedback, as has been previously discussed in this chapter, is readily available and is a critical learning tool when using drills. The ball flight information helps you know when you are achieving the desired results of the drill. The feel of the motion is matched with the desired results. Likewise, ball flight can help you determine what you are not doing. Therefore, you can learn from the ball flight and correct yourself. For example, if you are using the Hit and Hold Drill to create a delayed release and target-side awareness through impact, the desired ball flight is relatively low and boring, similar to the punch-shot results. If the ball flight is high and soft, this indicates an early release and flippy action due to the breakdown in your target side at or prior to impact. You have not accomplished the intended objective of the drill—yet! Keep trying!

Overuse Promotes Abuse

Drills are not designed to be used for long periods of practice time, so that hitting fifty to one-hundred balls using only one drill is not recommended. Overuse of a drill causes the drill to become a separate skill within itself. Yet the purpose of the drill is to help establish a desired feel within your total swing motion.

The drill helps separate a specific part of the swing. The part must always be put back into the whole swing motion or short game motion. It is suggested that the drill be used as directed for three to five swings and then the related swing feel be incorporated into the whole motion you are practicing.

Variety Adds Spice

There are numerous drills designed for specific aspects of the swing. Often, one drill may not be effective in helping you establish the desired feel. You may need to try several drills before you hit on one that triggers your particular need. Additionally, incorporating numerous drills for a specific need can add interest to your sessions by helping you maintain your motivation and concentration.

Consider Safety

Certain drills are not recommended for individuals who have some physical limitations. If you have lower back problems, target-shoulder dislocations, bad knees, bursitis or arthritis, or some other limitation, you need to consider the demands of the drill relative to your specific physical limitations. For example, one target-side awareness drill, Rear Hand Off After Impact, requires that the target arm swing through singly after impact. If your target shoulder is prone to dislocating, this drill is not recommended for you. There are other drills that accomplish the same thing and are safer for your use. If you do not have a shoulder problem, this drill is fine.

Accept the Challenge

Drills are fun and motivating. However, they can initially be very frustrating. Sometimes it takes only one or two tries to achieve the desired feel and results of the drill. Other times, it may take ten or more tries to be successful using a drill.

Using drills may be a new experience, but do not let the lack of immediate success deter your efforts. Anytime something new or different is tried, it takes time to adjust to the newness.

Take the Toe Drill (an arm-swing drill) as an example. This drill relates the arm swing to upper body dominance. In the drill, you are in the desired posture over the ball, balanced on one leg, with your other leg positioned directly behind and your foot balanced on your toe (Figure 6.1). If your upper body tends to be extremely active on the forward swing, this precarious position is intimidating. At first, you often feel unbalanced and out of control. In time, however, you can identify the cause of your imbalance, and with patience, you can begin to feel your arms rather than your shoulders.

The old adage "If at once you don't succeed, try and try again" is most fitting for those first drill tries. Consider the challenge and go for it!

PRACTICE AIDS

Practice aids are external devices such as shafts, 2 x 4s, or weighted clubs that provide additional feedback during your practice session. They can be used when working on drills and on your whole swing motion, when at the practice area or at home, when hitting balls, or when making practice swings.

Most practice facilities, pro shops, schools, and homes have some practice aids available. The "homemade" variety can be just as effective as those available commercially. Table 6.3 provides a reference for suggested aids and their use. The corresponding laws and principles (Chapter 2) for which they provide supplemental feedback during practice are indicated. This list is far from complete with respect to the potential numbers and types of aids available. Many of these aids are discussed in the next section in reference to their use with drills (part and whole motion).

As depicted in the chart, many practice aids serve similar purposes. Some may be more effective for you than others. Some may be more accessible than others. Because there are several options, however, cost should not be a limitation.

Figure 6.1. The Toe Drill may cause frustration when it is first tried.

Figure 6.2. The Swing Machine provides kinesthetic feedback to help you learn to "feel" your golf swing.

Table 6.3

Suggested Practice Aids—with corresponding laws and principles for which they can provide supplement feedback.

Practice Aids:	Laws						Principles														
	Speed	Path	Face	Angle of Approach	Squareness of Contact	Alignment	Weight Distribution	Grip	Posture	Ball Position	Swing Center	Balance	Release	Timing	Plane	Width of Arc	Length of Arc	Position—Top	Targets	Levers	Stance
Shafts/Clubs	•	•		•		•			•	•	•		•		•	•	•		•	•	•
2 × 4s		•		•		•	•		•	•									•		
Ball Buckets		•		•			•		•	•		•				•	•		•		•
Waterbase Paint		•	•			•	•			•									•		•
Tees		•		•		•				•			•						•		•
Towels	•												•								
Jump Ropes	•					•					•		•			•	•		•		
Mirror		•	•	•		•	•	•	•	•	•	•			•	•	•	•	•		
Your Shadow		•				•			•	•	•				•	•	•	•			
Reminder Grip			•	•				•													
Teacher Putter		•	•		•																
Weighted Club	•												•	•	•			•		•	
Whipping Shaft	•												•	•						•	
Swing Machine		•				•			•	•	•	•			•						•

DRILLS

The drills in this section are for specific aspects of the swing motion. General technique drills (i.e., for chipping, putting, etc.) have been provided in Chapters 3 and 4.

These drills are used for both developing and reinforcing feel awareness and technique in your swing. As such, they are not restricted to the practice tee. Many golfers use drills for warming up prior to play when they do not have time to hit balls; other golfers do drills on the course during play, while awaiting their shots, to establish a feel or to stay loose. Drills help you turn your thoughts away from technique and on to feel, yet the drills themselves are founded on sound technique.

Target-Side Awareness Drills

Purpose: To develop an awareness of the target-side role in the swing.

These drills are good for:
- Weak or inactive target side
- Overpowering rear side
- Deceleration through or at impact
- To feel a swinging motion rather than a hit
- To reduce tension (target or rear side)

Desired Ball Flight: On target with slight draw.

Rear Hand Off After Impact
A regular swing is made. Just after impact, the rear hand comes off, allowing the target hand and arm to continue swinging to the completion of the follow-through (Figure 6.3).

Initially, begin with slow-paced swings to develop timing, gradually working to full-paced swings. This drill can be used for both full and short game swings.

Note: If you have any problems with your target-side shoulder, do not use this drill.

Overlap
Take your regular grip. Slide your rear hand up over your target hand. Your rear hand will overlap your target hand so that none of your rear hand is on the club (Figure 6.4).
This drill is good for full and short game swings.

152

Figure 6.3. Rear Hand Off After Impact Drill develops target-side awareness.

Figure 6.4. The Overlap Drill helps develop strength in the target side.

Claw

Take your regular grip. Remove the index finger and thumb of your rear hand from the shaft. The shaft will extend between your middle and ring fingers. Your target hand and the three fingers of your rear hand will hold the club (Figure 6.5). Maintaining the interlock or overlap position your rear hand can be removed and placed above the shaft. Gradually add the rear hand fingers one by one to attain the regular grip position.

This drill is good for full and short game swings.

Hit and Hold

The regular full swing motion is made through impact. The swing is "checked" or stopped right after impact. Your arms do not go beyond hip height on the target side. Check to be sure your hands and arms are in front of the clubhead when the swing is stopped (similar to a punch shot under low-hanging trees).

Wide Whoosher

Grip the club in your target hand on the shaft just above the head. Hold the club in front of your body with your target-hand palm facing the ground. The grip end should point away from your target (or imaginary target). Extend your rear hand, gripping the club with your fingers, rear hand palm up. Your arms will be shoulder-width apart.

Holding the club, take your regular full swing posture with your arms hanging freely. Swing to the top of your backswing. As you start down, let go with the rear hand. Pull through with the target hand and arm (Figure 6.6). Be sure to incorporate your lower body in the drill. The swing motion will create a "whooshing" sound.

Figure 6.5. The Claw Drill helps develop target-side awareness, similar to the Overlapping Drill.

Figure 6.6. The Wide Whoosher Drill creates an awareness of target-side control and arm speed.

155

Figure 6.7. The rear hand position for Wide Whoosher establishes a feel for lower body motion.

To insure lower body motion, hold the club in your target hand. Place your rear hand on your back hip pocket (Figure 6.7). Using your target hand and arm, swing the club to the top of your swing. Just before you start your forward swing, push forward with your rear hand. Try to maintain your swing center during the swinging motion.

Arm and Hand Drills
Purpose: To develop an awareness of proper arm and hand motion in the swing.

These drills are good for:
- Weak or inactive arms and hands
- Improper use of arms and hands
- Developing an awareness of release
- Developing an awareness of forearm rotation
- Timing
- Developing an awareness of the role the arms and hands play in controlling swing pace.
- Overactive upper body

Desired Ball Flight: On target, slight draw.

Toe Drill
Take your regular full swing posture with an iron. Place your rear foot directly behind your target foot so that the rear foot is balanced on the toe (refer to Figure 6.7). The ball position is to the rear side of your target heel and the swing center is on the target side of the ball, which creates a descending angle of approach. Your weight should be on your target foot, from the midstep to the ball of the foot. In this position, make your regular full swing or mini-swings.

If your upper body tends to be overactive, you will feel an immediate loss of balance on the forward swing.

This drill can be reversed for us with woods. Your rear foot is the balance foot, with your target foot behind on the toe. The ball position is to the target side of your rear foot, and the swing center is to the rear side of the ball, which encourages a level to ascending approach.

Two Bucket
Place two ball buckets of the same height just less than shoulder-width apart (Figure 6.8). Stand on the buckets. Take a posture position in which your arms are hanging freely. Your club should brush the ground. Only make practice swings that are 1-to-1, 2-to-2, or 3-to-3 swing length. You should feel your arms working as a unit.

If you tend to raise up (active upper body), or collapse or bend your target arm, the club will not brush the ground.

157

Knee Time

Kneel on the ground, taking a knee stance (Figure 6.9). Using a wood, tee the ball up and make swings.

This drill promotes the arms to swing around the body. The arms and hands must work together, rotating back and through the ball.

If the shoulders are overactive, the club will bounce behind the ball. The shoulders remain fairly level as the arms control the motion and the body responds. The angle of approach is level.

Figure 6.8. The Two Bucket Drill develops a feel for arm freedom.

Figure 6.9. The Knee Time Drill promotes a sense of forearm rotation and hand action.

159

Bench Sit

Sit on the edge of a bench (Figure 6.10) or in a chair. Tee the ball up. Hit shots. You will be swinging in a manner similar to the knee shot. The purpose is the same.

Tee-Down to Tee-Down

Place a tee in the end of your grip (use 7- to 9-irons). Make 3-to-3 length swings. On the backswing and follow-through, the tee will point toward the ground.

Figure 6.10. The Bench Sit Drill, as does the Knee Drill, develops arm motion through rotation.

Arm and Hand Motion

Using an iron or wood, take your regular grip. Stand erect, with your feet shoulder-width apart (Figure 6.11). Extend your arms in front of your body with the clubhead pointing at an imaginary target. The club is in line with your arms (no angle is formed). Swing the club, making a backward and forward swing, with your arms and hands.

You want to feel the forearm rotation with the cocking-uncocking-cocking of the wrist. Shoulder involvement is minimal, which accentuates the feeling in the hands and forearms. Keep the arms fully extended as you swing, but feel the motion of your hands.

Figure 6.11. The Arm and Hand Motion Drill develops arm feel and understanding of the release.

161

Preset

Take your regular setup position, using a wood or an iron (Figure 6.12). Without moving your arms, preset your wrist cock. The club shaft will be pointing away from the target and parallel to the target line. Maintain this preset position and make your regular swings.

You should feel more of the arms controlling the swinging motion on the backward and forward swings. This drill is particularly good if you tend to be "wristy" with little arm control. It helps establish a feeling of maintaining the wrist cock longer on the forward swing, delaying the release and reducing the tendency to overuse your hands early in the forward swing.

Figure 6.12. The Pre-Set Position helps deactivate the hands and create an arm motion.

Leg Drills

Purpose: To develop a feel for the desired motion of the lower body as a support system during the swing.

These drills are good for:
- Lack of or ineffective lower body motion
- Rhythm
- Weight shift
- Timing

Knee Touch

Take your regular full swing setup position for a wood or iron. On your backswing, your target knee touches your rear knee; your rear knee touches your target knee on the forward swing. Your heels will come off the ground slightly during the swing. You should feel your weight shift on the backswing and forward swing. This drill exaggerates the lower body motion to create the feeling. In time, your knees will not actually touch. However, to initially feel the motion, allow your knees to touch.

Baseball

Take your regular fullswing setup position with an iron or wood. Slide your target foot over to your rear foot. Make your backswing. Hold. Return your target foot to its original position and swing through. This motion of the lower body is similar to a batter stepping into a pitch. You should feel the lower body lead the forward swing slightly ahead of the arms. This drill takes a little time to coordinate. You may initially want to try it with the ball on a tee. Have patience.

Rapid Fire

Line ten balls in a row, 2 inches apart. Take your regular setup position, standing 2 feet from the line of balls. The line of balls will be to the target side of center in your stance if you were addressing the first ball. Begin making full swings. Gradually moving toward the row of balls, continue swinging and hit the balls. Do not interrupt the motion. Make forward swings and backswings on the same path as you shift your weight from one side to the other. As you move forward, your weight shifts. On the backswing, your weight is on your rear foot. As you step forward with your target foot, the forward swing begins. As you step forward with your rear foot you begin the back swing a completion of the forward swing. Continue this steady motion until you finish the tenth ball.

You should feel a swinging motion back and through. This develops a rhythmic sensation with the weight shift. As you feel more

163

comfortable, try to be aware of your lower body leading the swing motion. This drill may take some time to feel coordinated. Again, have patience!

Partner Jam

Stand with your target foot 3 inches from your partner's rear foot. Take your regular setup position, without holding a club. Allow your arms to hang freely as you assume your posture. Make your full swing motion allowing your arms to swing freely without touching hands. As you start your forward swing, the lower body sequence should be target heel-knee-hip. Your target knee should hit or contact your partner's knee before your hips turn as you continue to swing through.

Make swings with a partner, then without, trying to create the same motion and feeling. Then hit balls with the same thoughts. Go back and forth between partner and no partner, hitting balls until it begins to feel more comfortable. This drill encourages you feel the lateral motion of your lower body. Lead by planting your target heel and driving your knee. If you tend to restrict your lower body motion or spin your hips in an attempted lower body motion, this drill is good for you. The newness of motion of your legs and swing may create a looseness or more relaxed feeling. This often produces some anxiety, which increases your upper body involvement. You may lose your timing. Stick with it. Control and distance will come.

Path Drills

Purpose: To develop a visual and kinesthetic awareness of the desired path in the swing.

These drills are good for:
- Inconsistent swing path
- Understanding ball flight
- Understanding arm motion in controlling the path

Desired Ball Flight: Varies, depending upon the drill.

Bench

Place a bench on its side, parallel and slightly outside the target line (See Figure 6.13). Make practice swings close to the bench to become sensitized to the object. Gradually move within 3 or 4 inches of the bench, and continue swinging. When you feel comfortable, place the ball 3 or 4 inches from the bench. Your clubface will be about an inch from the bench. When the ball is positioned, swing away.

The bench is initially intimidating. As you become accustomed to it, the bench will provide a visual guide for the club path back and through the ball. Club-bench contact will occur. Hit the bench a few times to feel the contact. It will not hurt. It provides immediate feedback!

Note: A three-foot 2″ x 4″, broken club shaft, regular club, jump rope, etc. are substitute aids. The bench is useful because it makes a bigger impression!

Object in Front or Behind

Place a ball, tee, or any small object 12 to 15 inches in front and/or behind the ball. Swing the club over the rear ball on the backswing and over the front ball on the forward swing.

Figure 6.13. The Bench Drill provides a visual aid for swinging the club on path.

165

Note: The objectives may vary with your need. For example, these path tendencies may suggest the following:

- Outside on backswing: Try to swing the club to the inside of the rear ball.
- Inside too much on backswing: Try to swing over or outside the rear ball.

This drill provides you with a visual guide for directing your swing path. Often when you try only to feel the path internally, the signals get jammed. The external path helps free your thoughts and direct your motion.

Target Guide

Place an umbrella or a broken shaft at least 21 feet from the ball and in line with a designated target (Figure 6.14). Hit balls to the right, left, or over the target.

The target provides a visual guide and feedback for ball flight. You can learn to maneuver the ball around objects using this guide. It allows you to practice your visualization techniques while improving your path control. It is fun in competition with yourself and with others.

Figure 6.14. The Target Guide provides an external visual guide for ball path.

Tee Path

With tees, paint, jump ropes, etc., outline the desired swing path your club should follow, depending upon your needs. Practice swinging along the created path and then hit balls along the same.

Angle of Approach Drills

Purpose: To develop an awareness of the desired ascending and descending angles of approach in executing various types of shots.

These drills are good for:
- Understanding angle of approach
- Overactive hands
- Early release
- Overpowering rear side

Desired Ball Flight: Depends upon the shot intent.

Single Bucket

Ascent—Take your regular full swing for a tee shot. Place a ball bucket under your target foot as illustrated in Figure 6.15. Make your regular full swings, hitting balls.

Ascending.   Descending.

Figure 6.15. The Single Bucket drills develop a feel for body position when delivering a descending or ascending angle of approach.

167

Descent—Take your regular iron full swing or mini-swing setup. Place a ball bucket under your rear foot as illustrated in Figure 6.15. Make full swings or mini-swings, maintaining this position.

These drills limit lower-body mobility while helping you maintain the position of the swing center throughout the swing. A position of the swing center in front of the ball encourages a feeling of descent with the arm and hand motion. The swing center behind the ball creates an ascending feeling.

Pencil Tee
Place the ball on the end of a pencil that is teed in the ground. Hit balls from the tee with a wood.

This is an excellent drill for helping you feel the ascending angle of approach with a drive. If your angle is too steep (overactive shoulders), the pencil is knocked out and the ball drops down. You must maintain a level-to-ascending arm swing motion.

2" x 4"
Take your mini-swing setup position. Place the 2" x 4" perpendicular to the target line, outside your rear foot. Make practice swings to feel the descending angle. The club should not hit the board. Hit balls with the board in position.

If you tend to release too soon, the club will hit the board. This drill helps you feel the release delay.

Summary
Plan ahead to make your practice sessions more fun and effective. A systematic approach to practice will help you improve your play performance while enjoying your practice. Remember: You play as you practice and practice as you play.

7

GOLFING OUT OF YOUR MIND

Golf is often thought to be half physical skills and half mental. How many times have you heard a golfer exclaim "I had the shots, but I just couldn't get the ball in the hole", or "I can't believe I choked on 8 and 9. I had great approach shots, but I couldn't find the green"; or "I just knew I would hit O.B. [out of bounds] on 6—everytime I see water I slice the ball!"

Such statements indicate that your mind is overpowering your physical skills. It happens to almost all golfers at one time or another. But you can control this state of mind, just as you can control your tendency to hook or slice the ball.

If you want to control your mind as well as your swing, the first step is to determine what influences your ability to strike the golf ball. If you have practiced well and carefully hit many golf balls, you should be able to execute the same shot during a round of golf that you hit on the practice tee. If you can't, then your emotions probably are getting in the way of your golf swing. Get out of the way of your swing!

If you have done your homework and had effective practice sessions, not "ball-beating session," then you should be able to execute on the course. If you can't, then let's find out why.

Take a minute or two to answer the following questions. Be honest—this is your chance to improve! Take the "Assert" Test. Assert yourself. Learn to read your own body and know when your thoughts and concerns are taking control of your golf swing.

Assert: A Swing Self-Evaluation—Tension Levels

Instructions: Circle the response that most agrees with your choice for each situation.

	Strongly Agree	Mildly Agree	Mildly Disagree	Strongly Disagree
1. When I have an important shot to make, my hands get cold and sweaty.	4	3	2	1
2. If my score on the first few holes is bad, the rest of my round is bad.	4	3	2	1
3. I am quite critical of myself.	4	3	2	1
4. I often second-guess myself and choose another club.	4	3	2	1
5. I would be happy to leave certain clubs in my car. I would rather not hit them anyway.	4	3	2	1
6. When I must hit over a sand trap I see the ball landing in the bunker.	4	3	2	1
7. When I get into trouble during a tournament, I try new shots that I have not carefully practiced.	4	3	2	1
8. I find myself holding my breath and sweating on important shots.	4	3	2	1
9. Sometimes I can't sleep well the night before a tournament.	4	3	2	1
10. I eat, smoke, or drink more before an important match.	4	3	2	1

Scoring Assert: Score your response to each question. Add each of your responses together to determine a total score.

Maximum score = 40   My total score =

Score	Assert Level
36-40	Excess tension
29-35	Above average tension
21-28	Average tension
14-20	Relaxed
10-13	Lethargic; very relaxed

Tension can negatively affect your golf performance. It doesn't matter whether your tension is real or imaginary. Your apprehension may be realistic ("I can't hit a straight shot from a tee with a driver more than three out of ten times") or it may be imagined ("I don't think I can hit this shot"). Your body will respond the same in either case.

When you become nervous about a golf shot, your body sends several signals to your mind. The muscles of your body will generally tighten. You will begin to breathe more rapidly. You probably will not be able to detect the subtle changes in the tension in your arms or shoulders. Your visual scanning will become narrower. You may gasp for air.

If you become tense enough, you can actually "choke to death." The phrase "I choked" is derived from this physiological response. In fact, many people who are thought to have drowned actually choked to death because they were so afraid.

The tense or anxious thoughts that you experience while playing golf may cause you to choke. The tension associated with critical decisions may cause you to miss important information, make "dumb" choices, or "yip" over putts.

The theory that you must get "psyched up" to play well may be untrue. Getting "psyched up" may mean getting "psyched out." You cannot get more and more "psyched up" and expect to play better and better. In fact, we now know that there is an intermediate level of excitement that produces the best results. You can not be too relaxed, nor can you be too intense.

The actual relationship between tension and performance is not linear. It is probably an "inverted U," in which a moderate level of tension produces the best results. For example, if you normally shoot an 82 (handicap about 10), you can expect to shoot that score when you are moderately anxious. If you are too excited, or too relaxed and lazy, you may shoot a 92. This inverted-U relationship between arousal and performance is shown in Figure 7.1.

Most golfers are overly anxious. You may try to accomplish too much, or expect too great a score. But great expectations can be overcome. You can learn to control your thoughts and tensions.

In order to learn to control your thoughts and tension, you must learn to "read" your mind and body. As you play a round of golf, your body communicates with you by sending signals about your respiration rate, heart rate, amount of sweat (perspiration), and the types of thoughts that possess you. By paying attention to these signals, you can learn to control your emotions.

"Listen" to your body when you are tired. For example, one sign of fatigue may be a loss of distance, such as hitting a 5-iron only 120 yards when you normally hit it 150 yards. When this happens, you rest, or choose a 4-iron if you need to go 150 yards.

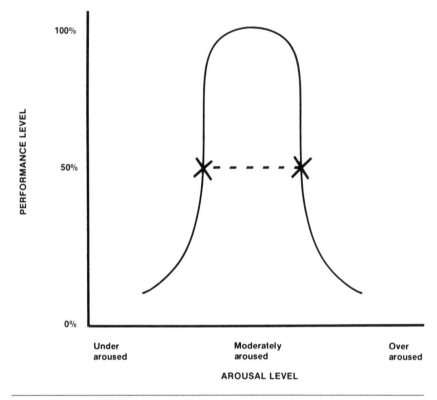

Figure 7.1. Inverted-U relationship between performance and arousal.

TENSION CONTROL

Learning to control your tension is like learning to putt, or to sink a freethrow in basketball. The first step is to recognize when you are tense or anxious.

Understanding your body and its communication system is not as easy as learning to hit a slight draw with a 7-iron. Our language sometimes fails us when we want to talk about how we feel. So let's develop a language to communicate about our bodies. We will establish a system to describe the range of behaviors that we can produce—let's call it the "system of 5s."

172

Using the System of 5s

Everything we do has a "happy medium." The old saying that "more is better" does not always hold. It is not always better to hit the ball harder (especially when you are trying to make a 2-foot putt). Nor is it better to "ease up," especially when you are playing a par 3 from 190 yards away. In the concept of 5s a 3 is assigned to the desired level. Beyond this level is a 4 or 5. Less than the desired level is a 1 or 2. In other words, if you grip the club at a specific tension, that is a 3. If you hold on too tightly (a gorilla grip) it is a 5. If you are "loosy-goosy" then it is a 1 or 2.

This system of 5s allows you to talk to yourself about your performance. If you are too tense, tell yourself you are a 5, back off until you are a 1, and then find the desired 3. If you are too loose at the top of your backswing, tell yourself you are a 1, and increase the tension until you become a 3.

You can use the system of 5s for any body part. You should be able to demonstrate the entire range of 1-5 in each area of the body: hands, arms, shoulders, length of backswing, speed of swing, hip rotation, leg action, alignment, and so on.

The system of 5s will allow you to talk to yourself or to others about golf. You can tell a friend that his/her swing has a tempo of 1 . . . and needs to speed up to a 3. Then, as the rate increases, you have a scale upon which to indicate improvement.

Manifestations of Tension

When you become tense and anxious, you will probably respond by becoming a 5 in many areas. You will probably grip the club tighter and therefore not let your hands release. The result will be a clubface error and a slice. You may also reduce the fluidity of your swing, therefore shortening the length of your swing and losing distance. And you may also fail to let the wrist cock effectively, therefore reducing the hand action and losing distance and control in your shots.

Golfers who can detect when they are tense, and those who can tell why they are tense, will have a tremendous advantage. If you see yourself slicing the ball and feel tension in your body, remind yourself that a 3 is the ideal level—not a 5. Listen to your body and hear it tell you if the problem is in your hands, wrists, arms, or legs.

Par Threes—The Tension Traps

Manifestations of tension and anxiety are present in many aspects of golf, perhaps most obviously on par 3s—the pesky little monsters of golf. Par 3s are the holes that give even the novice some hope of a birdie, and the holes that decide many championships. An historical look at par 3s emphasizes their importance in golf. Tom Watson's

173

chip shot on the par 3 seventeenth hole in the 1982 Open at Pebble Beach was depicted by most of the world as the epitome of golf. And there was the 1965 Masters Tournament 9-stroke win by Jack Nicklaus. At that tournament, Nicklaus was five under par on the par 3s (forty-three strokes)compared to the runner-up, who was four to five over par (fifty-two to fifty-three strokes). Those nine strokes on par 3s made the difference!

For the average golfer, par 3s are an even more complex problem. Most golfers have two major problems on par 3s: coming up short of the green and poor club selection. In fact, V. Farrell Thomas' six-year study (See References) showed that 63% of all tee shots on par 3s land short of the green. Almost none go beyond the green. These short shots are a sure indication of tension and its effect of shortening the distance obtained on drives.

Self-Control Technique

Several techniques may help control your tension. The most important one centers on control over your body. The rate at which you breathe sends many signals to your brain. When you get nervous or tense, you breathe faster. Therefore, if you can actively slow down your respiration rate, you can tell your brain that you are in control. Try the following Self-Control Technique.

Self-Control Technique:
- Say "stop"
- Take a deep breath
- Exhale
- Say "I'm in control"

Then replace your negative or self-doubting thought with a positive one: "I can make that putt; I have practiced that a hundred times . . . . "

CONTROLLING SELF-TALK

Have you ever listened to your self talk to yourself? If you haven't, try it some time. You might be surprised to know that winners say what they want to happen. Losers say what they fear might happen.

If you stand on the tee and tell yourself "Gosh, I hope I don't hit out of bounds on the right," or if you say "I can't afford to slice another one," you are focusing on the negative. Think about that big fairway down the middle. Preset your body to hit the ball where you want it to go.

Negative thoughts do two damaging things. They increase your body tensions and they focus your attention on the wrong thing rather than the correct one. If you start thinking about all of the bad things that can happen, they just might. "What ifs" may become "whiffs" and cost you important strokes.

Being positive does not mean fooling yourself. It requires that you know your strengths and weaknesses and play within them. Once you know your capabilities, you can choose the action that has the highest probability of success.

You must learn to control your self-talk. It takes practice, just like putting or chipping. Some young, elite players have been cruel to themselves during play. They may say very negative and even demeaning things to themselves. Sometimes when their play grows worse, their self-talk becomes even more negative, causing their play to become even worse. Such golfers will never become great unless they break out of this vicious cycle!

The first step in controlling self-talk is to recognize what you say to yourself and when. You may need to carry a small tape recorder with you and talk out loud into it during a round of golf. Or fill your right pocket full of paperclips and everytime you say something negative move a clip into your left pocket. One professional golfer tried this technique and found eighty-three paper clips in her left pocket after eighteen holes of golf. That's eighty-three paper clips in her left pocket after eighteen holes of golf. That's eighty-three negative, self-defeating thoughts! And her score was even more than 83! The objective is to turn those self-defeating thoughts into self-enhancing ones. Imagine how much better you might play if you said eighty-three good things (or even neutral things) to yourself rather than negative words or images.

If you wish to control those negative thoughts, use the Self-Control Technique. Say "stop"; take a deep breath; say "relax"; exhale; say "I'm in control" and "I can . . . ." The final phrase of the technique should be what you can and want to do, not what you fear you might do.

For example, if you said "look at that big O. B. on the right," you should then use the Self-Control Technique and finish by saying "I'm in control; I can easily hit it into the fairway that's about 35-yards wide. I have done it many times in practice." This positive statement will focus your attention on the target landing area, allow your body to relax, and allow your thoughts to "get out of the way" of your swing.

Coping Techniques

It is often a good idea to anticipate any problems that may arise and then practice how you will deal with them. This technique is called "coping practice" and can be used for both physical and

175

psychological practice. The physical practice techniques described in Chapter 3 suggest that you practice in the "extremes" in order to find the "means" to better technique. You must also practice coping with "mental errors" or self-defeating thoughts.

Coping techniques require that you identify your strengths and weaknesses, and those things that bother you. We know that there are generally four conditions which may cause you to be anxious.

Sources of Anxiety
- Ego Threat
- Threat of social evaluation
- Fear of the unknown
- Disruption of routines

The first two sources of anxiety relate to a desire to be successful. Sometimes we measure this success by our ability to do as well as we had planned. When we do not do as well as we expect, we may be disappointed with ourselves. This is a form of ego threat.

Other golfers are more motivated by what they think others will feel about them. This concern over what others think produces a special kind of anxiety, called a threat of social evaluation. When a family member or professional colleague is watching, do you feel excess tension and worry about what they may think?

Some golfers become quite tense when they do not know what to anticipate. If you have to play on a new course, or with new partners in your foursome, it may cause you to be tenser than usual. This source of fear can be easily tempered. Go out to the course the day before, or at least an hour or so before your tee time. Walk the course, check for distances and intermediate targets. The more familiar you are with the course, the more relaxed you will play.

The last type of stressor is related to having your own personal habits disrupted. You may always like to have a shower in the morning before you play, or you may like to chew gum when you play. If these are disrupted, you may not feel at ease when you play. In order to combat this source of stress, you must either provide a backup system so that they are not disrupted, or you must learn to cope with them as a potential disruption.

In order to successfully conquer your fears and frustrations, you must practice performing under stressful conditions. You must identify those things that cause you to respond emotionally with negative and anxious thoughts, and then rehearse coping with these thoughts. You should practice dealing with any anxiety-provoking situations that may occur during your golf rounds. Think carefully about all types of anxiety-provoking situations and make a list of them. List everything that might affect your thoughts and concentration.

**Recognize Your Own
Potential Anxiety Provokers**

- Poor golf-course conditions
- Poor weather
- Minor injury
- Lost or damaged clubs
- Misplaced lucky piece
- Lost ball marker
- Obnoxious golfer in foursome
- Poor housing or food
- Unsophisticated or noisy audience
- Distractions from family or friends
- Outside business distractions
- Undesirable tee-off time
- Play delays due to weather
- Missing several putts in a row
- Failing to play well on the first day
- Opponents who try to psych you out
- Poor practice round

Once you have identified the situations that may be a problem for you, use the Self-Control Technique and rid yourself of the distraction. Anticipate what can happen and practice dealing with it.

Mastery Technique
When you are ready to test your skill, to compete in a tournament or "play for real," you must become a positive thinker. It is important to practice coping with problems, self-doubts, and negative thoughts. But as you prepare to compete, you must be a "maximizer." Take advantage of your strengths and positive thoughts.

When you are ready to tee it up, and for several days before a big round, you must be a self-enhancer. Winners see what they want to happen. Imagine those putts sinking. Hear and see the ball drop.

Mastery and Coping Tapes
One effective practice strategy for dealing with "mind mastery" is to make audio tapes of your self-talk. One tape should be for coping rehearsal. In it you should describe several "problem" thoughts or

situations and then effectively cope with them. This tape can be played at home or as you drive to work, school, or shopping. Listen to yourself become a self-enhancer.

The mastery tape should be played immediately prior to competition. In this case it is important to initially see yourself being successful, even in difficult situations.*

IMAGERY CONTROL

Your mind exerts a powerful influence on your body. It is sometimes hard to distinguish what you have imagined from what is real. Some mornings you may wake up and not remember if that dream was real or not. Did you really have that conversation or actually shoot 2 under par?

If your mind is that convincing, perhaps you can use it to your advantage. If you can visualize, feel, smell, and see a good golf drive, then you have a better chance of executing one. Stand on the tee and imagine hitting a beautiful drive. Your muscles will feel it, your "mind's eye" will see it, and you will be ready to hit it.

A good imagination can give you a head start on your swing. If you systematically allow your mind to rehearse a swing, then when you physically hit the ball it's your second shot. You can hit the ball a second time without counting it as a stroke! You have already determined your alignment, intermediate target, stance, and swing. Now you are reviewing it for a second time.

Imagery

There are two basic forms of imagery, external and internal. The external form involves visually imagining yourself executing a shot. See yourself as if you were on film. Watch your whole swing and appreciate its beauty and fluid motion. See the ball go exactly where you planned it to go. This external imagery is as if you were watching yourself on TV.

Now try looking from inside your body. Look down your arms and hands to the ball. Notice your alignment, the position of the ball, the intermediate target. Now swing the club and see it contact the ball. See the ball fly down the fairway and land at the desired target. Notice the trajectory of the ball (Figure 7.2).

A sample copy of a mastery and coping tape can be obtained by writing: Dr. Linda Bunker, Ruffner Hall, Univ. of Virginia, Charlottesville, VA, 22903.

Figure 7.2. Look from inside your body.

Internal imagery involves your ability to sense what is going on in your body when you hit a golf ball. The 5s technique will help you develop this internal imagery. Feel your grip, the lightness in your fingers. Feel the slight tension across your back at the top of your backswing. Feel your hands release as the club returns to the contact point.

Both of these forms of visual imagery will allow you to rehearse your shots. Most beginners start by seeing themselves as if they were watching a television screen (external imagery). Later they develop the capacity to look from the inside to the outside, to allow their mind's eye to see down the club (internal imagery) and watch the ball travel just as it will with the actual shot.

Your imagery practice should center around positive performances. Picture and feel the tempo of your swing. Imagine a perfect shot. Then, when you step up to the ball, you will be confident that you can hit it well because you have practiced it many times in your mind.

Practice Swings

The value of a practice swing is that it presets your muscles to swing in the desired way. The swing should include an imaginary ball, a desired target area, and an up-to-tempo swing. A slow-motion swing can relax you but it won't allow you to practice the real swing. Find a target, set your clubface, and swing, just as you would if the ball were in place. Make your practice swing as real as possible.

Practice swings can also be effectively used after a real shot. If you hit the ball poorly, stand there and reswing the club. The poor shot would have been stored on your mind's "video-tape." Instead, you want to erase it by replacing it with another swing. In contrast, if you hit the ball well, stand there and let the video tape replay—remember how it felt and looked. Do not take a practice swing after a good shot, just let the image of that good shot be replayed.

CONTROLLING YOUR ATTENTION

The game of golf requires that each performer be able to control both their tension and attention. Your ability to control tension is related to your capacity to detect stressors and utilize effective coping techniques. Your ability to carefully direct your attention is merely another form of mental skill.

You must be able to concentrate when it is important. It would be very difficult to concentrate completely for every minute during a 4 1/2 hour round of golf. Instead, most good golfers are able to pay attention and concentrate when when it is important, and to let themselves go when it doesn't matter.

Your focus of attention must change many times during a round. In particular, there are two types of attention control needed: direction and width.

Direction of Attention:
- Internal = thoughts, feelings, and abilities.
- External = outside influences, characteristics of the course, climate, playing conditions, etc.

Width of Attention:
- Narrow = a single object or thought
- Broad = many different elements

Direction of attention must shift from external to internal thoughts. Imagine preparing to hit a ball 150 yards from a green. You must consider the external characteristics of the green, the landing area, traps, course conditions, etc. You must also consider your internal capabilities and control. Which club should you select? How easily can you control the ball from this location? Are you relaxed and ready to execute the shot?

180

The width of your attentional scanning must also shift during your preparation for a shot. You must initially gather all of the necessary information, from both external and internal sources. Then you must narrow your focus of attention to the specific task at hand—hitting that ball 150 yards.

The first step in a successful shot is to maintain a broad external focus in order to gather all of the necessary information about the particular shot. Then you must match those characteristics with your own capabilities by examining your own skills and abilities (a broad internal focus). Then you must select the correct club (narrow external focus). As you begin to set up for the shot, you must focus on the target (narrow internal focus). If you prefer to use an intermediate target (1/2 to 2 feet ahead of the ball), you must align your swing through the intermediate point to the final target (narrow external focus).

Once you have executed the shot, your attention must shift again. Watch the results of your swing. Notice where the ball lands, and how it flew through the air (narrow external focus). Capture the feelings associated with that shot, and rerun them in your mind so that you can store them (narrow internal focus). You may then wish to analyze the shot for its effectiveness compared to how you had planned it (broad external focus). Then visualize and feel the correct swing so that it will become automatic in the future (narrow internal focus).

Sequence of Attention for an Effective Golf Shot:
1. Broad external focus—to gather information
2. Broad internal focus—to examine personal skills
3. Narrow external focus—to select club
4. Narrow external focus—target orientation
5. Narrow internal focus—feel the shot
6. Narrow external focus—find intermediate target and alignment
7. Hit the ball
8. Narrow external focus—watch ball flight
9. Narrow internal focus—store the feel of the correct shot
10. Broad external focus—analyze shot

The attention shifts within one golf swing are many. They must be practiced just as you practice putting on different surfaces or from different locations. The shifts generally move from broad to narrow, and from external to internal. If you should be focusing on how the shot will feel, but find that your mind is still considering where you should land the ball, you must stop, regain control, and begin your routine again.

USING A ROUTINE TO FOCUS ATTENTION

The importance of a well-practiced routine must be reemphasized. Your pre-swing routine will help you relax, gather all the important information about the shot, and then "get out of the way." Your swing should be almost automatic. Do not start thinking about it in the middle of the execution. You must make all the important decisions ahead ot time, and then trust your body to execute. This confidence in your swing will be acquired as you practice using attention control coupled with good decision making.

You may wish to use a waggle as part of your routine. This pre-swing action of the hands and arms may help you relax. Ben Hogan has suggested that one of the main functions of the waggle is to teach you the "feel" of the upcoming shot. If this feel is to be obtained, the waggle must reflect the rhythm of the actual shot. Using a waggle in addition to your attentional routine may help you create a pattern that is easily repeated.

A good routine will allow you to maintain control. Some golfers hit one bad shot and it ruins their entire round. You must not allow that to happen. You must live in the present, not in the past or future. Remember: Yesterday is done, it's a canceled check; tomorrow is a promissory note, not good for much; while today is cash on the line!

Do not let yourself get mad or angry. If you allow your emotions to run away, you will only lose control. Remember that anger is only one letter short of danger. When you are upset, you will certainly be in danger of poor performance.

BREATH CONTROL

Whenever you feel tense or out of control, use your routines and self-control techniques to regain composure. One of the simplest techniques is breath control. When we talked of choking (an obvious breath-control problem) we emphasized that tension is related to breath control.

When you take a deep breath, you are telling your body that you are back in control. Take a deep slow breath, and feel yourself regaining control. Remember that the most important aspect of breath control is the forced exhalation. If you exhale vigorously, you will be able to produce more force. This improved force production is easily heard in the martial arts—performers yell as they exert force. As you strike a golf ball, you should remember to breathe out, not hold your breath. Try exhaling vigorously and you may be surprised at the added distance in your drives.

RELAXATION TRAINING

Breath control is one important aspect of relaxation. Feeling relaxed will induce a sense of calm, self-control, and attention focus. A total strategy for relaxation must be practiced just like any other skill.

Modified Progressive Relaxation

Many techniques have been developed to help you learn to relax. One of the most popular and successful techniques was originally developed by Dr. Edmund Jacobson. He emphasized recognizing and releasing unnecessary muscle tension. In order to do that, he developed a technique for exaggerating the body's tension and then releasing it. This technique is part of the system of 5s discussed in this book. You must learn to exaggerate tension — level 5 — and then learn to completely release it — level 1. The optimal level (3) can then be attained.

It is as important to experience the passive release and complete relaxation of level 1 as it is to know the total tension of level 5. To practice this, gradually tighten your fist and hold it for about six seconds. This level 5 tension represents your maximum level. Become aware of this high level of tension in each muscle group. Having held your fist to a 5 for six seconds, slowly release it until it is completely relaxed to a 1. Now make a fist to level 3, then 2, then 4, then 1. Learn to find each spot just like you can find a 1-1 swing length vs. a 3-3 swing length.

Learning total relaxation requires that you be able to locate any part of your body that has tension. Most golfers try to scan their body for tension and when it is found, say R-E-L-A-X. Imagine that your breath is being brought into a tense area and when you relax, you exhale the air and the tension. This sensation should leave you completely relaxed.

Locating areas of your body that have excess tension should be a systematic process. To practice, lie down on a smooth surface. Imagine yourself scanning each body part. Start with your feet and work up to your head. Feel your breath moving into your toes and feet. If you can, try the differential technique of first exerting a strong contraction (level 5) in your feet and legs, and then totally relaxing. Then check your upper legs and buttocks. You should be able to

183

scan through your entire body. Be sure that your back is relaxed, your arms, shoulders, neck, and forehead. Take many deep breaths and forced exhalations. You should be able to work through this routine on your own, or use an audio tape to help you.*

After you have learned to completely relax yourself, you should be able to combine it with the system of 5s. When you are relaxed, you should be able to create any level of desired tension. Some golfers systematically make their hands and arms a 2, then 3, then 4, then return to a level 3 before they swing. This form of controlled tension may be quite good for your swing. You may also find that visual imagery is enhanced when you are more relaxed. In order to feel your body, it is important to have a smooth baseline. Then you will be able to detect the subtle changes in tension, rhythm, and speed that may be important to your swing.

Body Relaxation Exercises

Controlling your body is important on the course and in preparation for play. There are several relaxation techniques that could be used, but perhaps the best starting place is attaining complete relaxation in a quiet environment.

The following format may help you learn to relax. Find a quiet place and lie down. Close your eyes, but do not force them shut. Relax. Tense all the muscles in your lower body, from your toes to your hips. Feel the tension as you hold it for sixteen seconds. Then say to yourself, " Relax, let go." Concentrate on your toes, lower legs, and buttocks. Your toes should point upward when tensed and flop to the outside when relaxed.

Now concentrate on your stomach. Tighten it and hold for one . . . two . . . three . . . four . . . five . . . six seconds. Then relax, let go. Repeat the word "relax" as you exhale. Then move to your fingers and through your shoulders. Tighten your arms and shoulders to a count of six. Then relax. Let your arms drop, your fingers spread, and completely relax. Feel your hands and arms. They should feel warm as they relax—not cold and clammy the way they may feel when you are tense or anxious. Remember this warm, relaxed feeling and learn to create it even when you are on the tee.

These relaxation techniques should be repeatable during a round of golf. You must be able to sense tension in your body and then control it. Practice with your arms and shoulders very tense (level 5).

Sample audio tapes of relaxation techniques are available by writing to: Linda Bunker, Ruffner Hall, Univ. of Virginia, Charlottesville, VA, 22903.

Note what happens when you strike the ball. If your arms and hands are too tight, the ball will generally slice and you will lose distance. Then practice with very loose arms and hands. The ball will probably hook slightly. These signs can be used to tell you when you are too tense during a round of golf. Recognize the signs and learn to control them by practicing these relaxation techniques.

The key to effective golf may be in learning to control your mind. Your body is a great tension barometer. If you can learn to recognize your tension producers, and then learn to reduce their manifestations, your golf game will improve dramatically. Key techniques include attention control, recognizing anxiety provokers, and learning to relax. Practice the techniques discussed in this chapter and your golf-game success rate will improve.

8

PRACTICE STRATEGIES FOR MENTAL CONTROL

All skills, both physical and mental, need to be practiced. The time spent on the practice tee and course should include physical aspects of your golf swing and course management. It should also include serious practice of the mental skills of golf. Learning to control your attention, to concentrate, to keep your anxiety under control, to utilize a routine, and to incorporate positive self-talk and imagery into your game all require practice.

TENSION MANAGEMENT

It is essential that you know how to detect excess tension and then learn to control it. Body tension may cause several different things to happen to your golf swing. In order to understand the effect of tension, practice hitting golf balls while tense. Using the system of 5s described earlier, hit several balls with different levels of tension in each body part.

Hit five golf balls under each of the following conditions. Notice the result in the flight of the golf ball.
- Grip very tight (5) vs. very loose (1).
- Shoulders very tight (raised toward ears) (5), vs. very loose (1).
- Legs tense, with little rotation (5), vs. legs loose (1).
- Total body tense (causing you to stand up straighter than usual) vs. a loose and relaxed body (1).
Experiment with different tension levels in each pair of body parts.

For example:
- 5 in the right hand, 3 in the left.
- 3 in the left, 1 in the right.
- 5 in the right shoulder, 3 in your left.
- 5 in your body, 1 in your hands and arms.

What did you notice as you hit those balls? When your hands were particularly tense, you probably did not release through the ball. The result of tension in the hands and arms is usually a slice, because you commit a clubface error. Remember those laws, principles, and preferences. They will help you correct your own problems.

What happened when the tension was in your posture? You probably stood up straighter, and may have topped the ball. When you had excess tension in your shoulders, you may have changed the path of your swing because of the excess involvement of the upper body.

Identify your ideal tension level. Once you know precisely how much tension you wish to develop, you will be able to monitor it and adjust your body accordingly. If you tend to grip your club too tightly when you get nervous or tense, you may wish to stand over the ball and consciously increase the tension in your grip and then relax it back to the desired level. For example, one golf professional from Holland counts to himself, two, three, four, three. He grips his club at a 2, increases beyond the desired level, and then settles in at his ideal 3 level.

Another good way to develop control is to work with a partner. Have your partner give you directions. For example, your partner might tell you to take a 3 grip and a 4 shoulder tension. Then both you and your partner should watch the result of your shots. The next command might be to take a 5/3 grip (right/left hands) and a very short (2) swing. That shortened swing may also be an indication of tension. Or your partner may tell you to swing very fast (5) and with a great deal of tension (5). Try every possible combination until you can produce each tension level in every body part.

Once you can induce tension at will, you will be able to relax at will. After all, if you can do a 1 to 5, you can relax to a 3. You might even wish to combine this technique with the thought control techniques. You may say to yourself "stop . . . relax . . . be a 3 . . . ." This is a very effective technique for some golfers.

Challenging Yourself

Some tension provokers are built into golf. Your tension may be raised if your ball lands in someone else's divot, if you are near a tree, if there is a loud crowd or noisy area. You must practice controlling these tension situations. Try the following drills.
- Hit your golf ball from a divot.
- Have a friend stamp down on your ball.
- Place your ball one clubhead length from a bench or board (Figure 8.1).

188

- Place your ball between two tees and then strike the ball without hitting the tees.
- Ask someone to verbally harass you while you are swinging.

Practicing under such stress conditions will help you when you actually face such situations. Let your imagination wander. What things really bother you? Once you have identified them, devise a practice situation so that you can learn to deal with them.

Figure 8.1. Place a ball next to a bench to gain tension control.

189

ENVIRONMENTAL STRESSORS

Some stressors in golf relate to the nature of the course or the weather. Some golfers love to play on wide open courses, others prefer tight fairways and greens. You must be able to play on both courses, so you must practice in both situations.

Imagine yourself standing in a tee-box of one of the most beautiful courses in the world. Look down that fairway and picture yourself about to tee off. Now transfer that image to your practice tee (Figure 8.2). Identify some landmarks that you can use to simulate that tight fairway. Imagine that you are really hitting down that beautiful scene each time you strike the ball. Another time, imagine that the practice tee is a wide open space so that you can swing away. Similarly, imagine a bunker directly between you and your 200-yard target. Or imagine a dogleg left or right. The more variety in your practices, the better.

Good golf course driving ranges will have a variety of targets or markers spread out in the range. These markers should help you develop your ability to concentrate and aim. If your practice area does not have such markers, you must be able to identify tufts of grass, weeds, or others landmarks. Or better yet, ask the range

Figure 8.2. Transfer an image of the course to the practice tee.

manager to place some objects in the open space. Such markers can be flags, old tires, Hula hoops, ropes, sheets, or almost anything else.

Weather Conditions

Golf is played in almost all weather conditions. You must practice in a variety of conditions so that you will be able to play in them. Do you know whether it is better to hit harder into the wind or with the wind? Is it better to select a club with more loft or less loft if the wind is blowing in your face? Can you concentrate when there is a strong sideward wind?

In order to answer these questions, you must have practiced in the wind. You must also practice in the rain. One successful coach told me that he carried around a squirt gun that shot a fine mist. Periodically during practice he would "shoot" his golfers so that they could learn to deal with that distraction. It might be a fun way in which to practice.

LEARNING TO CONTROL YOUR ATTENTION

Being able to concentrate on your golf game is a key to successful golf. It is important to be concentrating on your game every time you hit the ball. But is it necessary to be concentrating every minute of your round? Probably not. It is rather difficult to hold your undivided attention for over 4 1/2 hours. But it is essential to pay attention while you are hitting each of those shots.

One of the best techniques for focusing your attention is to use a careful routine. By establishing a consistent pattern of setup, alignment, and attentional direction, you will be able to concentrate at the critical moments.

Using a Routine

You should establish a precise routine. Just as a good basketball free-throw shooter always bounces the ball the same number of times before shooting, you should have a habit that you repeat before each of your golf shots. You should always take your grip at the same time and relative place, seek your alignment from the same place relative to the ball and the target, set your feet in the same order, etc. This stable routine will serve you well. It will provide you with a common base upon which to hit each and every shot.

Most good golfers have such a stable routine. Their routine follows the same order with each shot, and consumes the same amount of time. Many great golfers believe their routine is a critical part of their shots. If someone distracts them during their routine, they will start completely over—including drawing the desired club out of their bag.

Once you have stopped near the ball and your bag is in place to draw a club, you must "tune in" to your golf game. Don't feel guilty if your mind wanders while you are moving from one shot to the next. But once you are there, tune in by using your preestablished routine and the Sequence of Attention discussed in the last chapter, and reviewed here.

Sequence of Attention for an Effective Golf Shot
1. Broad external focus—to gather information
2. Broad internal focus—to examine personal skills
3. Narrow external focus—to select club
4. Narrow external focus—target orientation
5. Narrow internal focus—feel the shot
6. Narrow external focus—intermediate target and alignment
7. Hit the ball
8. Narrow external focus—watch ball flight
9. Narrow internal focus—store the feel of the correct shot
10. Broad external focus—analyze shot

Intermediate Targets

You can help your focus of attention by using an intermediate target. The same target you may have used to help alignment can focus attention. If you determine your ultimate target and then focus on the intermediate target, you will be able to tune in on your shot.

COMMUNICATING WITH YOURSELF

The way in which you talk to yourself can have a tremendous effect on your ability to play. We tend to believe ourselves, so if you repeatedly tell yourself how stupid you are, you may start to believe it. Instead, tell yourself to relax and to play within your abilities—you will do much better.

Controlling Your Self-Talk

The first step to effective self-communication is to control your self-talk. Be prepared to restructure your own personal conversations if you are generally a negative talker. The self-defeating effect of negative thinking is obvious in most sports. Instead, be a self-enhancer by saying positive, goal-directed things to yourself.

One way to practice positive self-talk is to record everything you say to yourself during a round of golf. Notice what you say, when you say it, and what it focuses upon. For example, you may stand on the tee and say "Look at that terrible O.B. on the right. If I hit over there I am really in trouble." If this is your last thought before you hit the ball, you are likely to get into trouble. Instead, identify the potential trouble, but then focus on what the successful shot must be. Do not dwell on the negative.

Using the thought-stopping technique described in the previous chapter will help. Each time you have a negative thought, say "stop," relax, and replace the negative thought with a positive one. The same technique can work if you are seeing negative things in your imagination. Replace them with a positive image.

Think for a moment about your own self-talk. Do you tend to say negative things to yourself? Do you set yourself up for success or for failure? Do you make excuses for yourself? Do you talk yourself out of practicing your poorer shots? Be honest. Recognize where you may have problems, practice to overcome them, and then feel good about your ability.

Believe in your ability to improve. Positive thinking is the one key to your golf game, but it is not the only one. You must be honest with yourself. Know yourself, don't snow yourself! Learn to read your anxieties, and cope with the stress.

Begin by making a list of all of the self-defeating or distracting thoughts that typically occur in a round of golf. Then practice changing those negative thoughts to self-enhancing ones. Keep the self-enhancing ones in the present tense, and phrased very personally. For example, if you would tend to say, "I do not play well with others who have higher handicaps," say "stop" and "I govern my own play in golf. The play of others does not bother me." Or if you might say "I don't play well in the wind, especially on a tight course," say "stop" and "I will just have to slow down and review each shot. Everyone must play in the wind, and I have hit more accurate balls on the range than will be required on these fairways." If you acknowledge how well prepared you are, and that everyone else must play under the same conditions, you may be able to make these initial fears into positive, confidence-inducing factors rather than excuse-generating ones.

Swing Thoughts

Some golfers talk to themselves too much. If you are overly analytic or make too many specific comments as you are swinging, you will detract from your skill. It is essential that you say good things when you do talk, but do not think that you must always be talking to yourself.

A single swing thought can be very helpful to your game. Most good golfers try to take their address position, and then think only of the total swing. Do not try to identify body actions or movements during your swing. Rather, choose one word to be your cue to effective swings. Choose a word that describes the feeling of the swing (swish, oily, ball, fly, etc.). Some golfers choose a word that relates to their goal. For example, one teenager uses the word "Australia" because he sees himself hitting the ball below the equator, and says —good-bye Australia.

You my also wish to experiment with a nonword. For example, try humming a single pitch. As you swing, the pitch should remain the same. If it changes in volume or pitch, you can suspect that your tension level is changing throughout your swing. Other techniques to measure tension can include counting by twos or threes. Or try counting backward from 99 by threes. Each of these techniques can be beneficial. They can serve to "distract" a small part of your attention, and they can prevent you from having other, more negatve thoughts.

COMBINING IMAGERY AND SELF-ENHANCEMENT

Being confident only comes when you feel competent. Developing competence requires knowing your strengths and weaknesses. Once you know what your capabilities are, you can prepare to meet any situation.

Using your imagination allows you to practice each situation ahead of time. Before each shot, visualize what a successful shot will look like. You should also feel that shot. Then, when you actually swing the club at the ball, you will have a good sense of what it should feel like. You should also combine this imaginary technique with practice swings. This will allow you to match the feel of your swing with the desired outcome.

Matching the real with the imaginary takes practice. You should spend time on the tee hitting golf balls and then storing the feeling of each hit. A good practice sequence would be to:

- Imagine a specific target.
- Imagine how the selected shot will feel.
- Imagine how the resultant ball flight will look and where the ball will land.
- Take a practice swing.
- Match the feel of that swing to your imagined swing.
- Actually hit the ball.
- Match the resultant hit with the practice feeling of the hit.
- Match the actual results of the swing with the imagined results.

If the actual swing was like the imagined one, good. If the result is different, determine why and repeat the sequence.

If you are playing a round of golf, use a practice swing, imagine the shot, and then hit the ball. If the result was good, take a moment and savor the feeling. If the shot was not effective, reimagine it or take a second practice swing. You must replace the poor feeling with a good one.

The ability to match stored images and feelings with desired outcomes is the key to success. You must be able to recall what a good shot was like before you hit the next one. This requires practice, the use of a solid, well-established routine, and the self-enhancement strategies previously discussed.

Another technique to help with your imagery practice is to develop a special image for a particular shot. For example, think of the action of the ball as a spank. If so, picture the ball as a "little bottom" ready to be spanked. Or when you are in the sand, you may wish to remind yourself that you need to hit the sand rather than the ball. Imagining the ball as the yolk of a fried egg may help you swing through the entire ball.

Another good practice technique for mental control is to focus on the hole when putting. Many good putters tell us that, just before they putt, the size of the hole begins to grow. They clearly see the path of the ball into the hole, almost as if they had carved an imaginary groove into the green. Wait until you see that path and roll the ball along it. Try not to think of actively hitting the ball. Caress it along the path.

Total Golf

The ability to use both your mind and body in golf is essential. You must practice skills in both areas. Learn to control your mind and to use it to your advantage, rather than allowing your mind to control your game.

9

PLAYING STRATEGIES AND COURSE MANAGEMENT

Up to this point you have been learning how to most effectively practice the physical and mental skills necessary to play better golf. Now it is time to learn the most effective way to apply those skills to actual playing conditions.

To best apply the skills you have learned in practice to playing a round of golf requires developing course strategy, or an understanding of course management. This is your plan for playing each hole. Each golf hole and each shot should be viewed separately. The following guidelines will help you develop a more systematic approach to course strategy.

ABCs of Course Strategy:
- Always select the route first.
- Be sure to select your club carefully.
- Composure during execution is essential.

SELECTION OF THE ROUTE

Stand on the tee and look down the fairway to the green (Figure 9.1). Your focus of attention should be directed at the target and away from yourself. Try to place yourself in the picture (Figure 9.1) and allow your self-thoughts to fade out while you concentrate on the goal of this hole. You should ask yourself the following questions.
- What is par?
- What is the length of the hole?
- Where are the strengths and weaknesses of the hole?
- How far is it to the fairway bunkers?
- How far is it to the water?

197

- Is the out of bounds a problem?
- How wide is the fairway?
- Which side of the fairway has the best opening to the green?
- Should I hit a wood or an iron?

These questions may initially seem overwhelming, but they are all important to helping you decide where and how to hit your tee shot and each successive shot.

Standing on the tee, you preplan your target areas for playing the hole. You must plan each shot, "see" each shot, "see" each landing area, and ultimately "see" the drop into the cup. The following three steps will help you determine the best way to preplan your route to the green.

- Identify and understand your individual strengths and weaknesses.
- Identify and understand the hole's strengths and weaknesses.
- Match your strengths with the hole's weaknesses.

Figure 9.1. Selecting a desired route is essential. You should focus attention on the intermediate and final targets.

Identify Individual Strengths and Weaknesses

The first step is a major one. Recognizing strengths is usually easy. Recognizing weaknesses is much harder. The suggested practice techniques in chapter 6 through 8 are designed to help you develop your strengths while improving upon your weaknesses.

With productive practice techniques and actual playing experience you develop an understanding of your swing tendencies, strengths, and weaknesses. An awareness of these tendencies, or "knowing thyself," is important to becoming a better player. Ask yourself the following questions.

- Do I have a consistent and directed pre-swing routine?
- How far do I hit each club?
- Is my normal ball trajectory high or low?
- What is my normal curvature? Right or left?
- What is my normal swing response in anxious situations? Relaxed or tense? Quick or slow?

If you can answer these questions, you are on the way to "knowing yourself." This requires a realistic assessment of your present abilities—strengths and weaknesses. These questions should become your guide in shot selection as you develop your strategy for each hole.

Identify the Hole's Strengths and Weaknesses

A golf hole is to an architect as a painting is to an artist. A golf hole is designed aesthetically and each is unique. The length, terrain, naturalness of its setting, woods, water, traps, and size of the greens—all add to the beauty and to the challenge. Some holes present greater challenges than others.

The greatest strengths of a hole are such designated trouble areas as hazards, out of bounds, trees or woods, tightness of fairways, narrow openings to greens, and small greens. These trouble areas may present themselves as penalty strokes in hazards or out of bounds, or as difficult shots from the woods or high rough.

The weaknesses of a hole are in contrast to the hole's strengths—they are free of potential penalties and trouble. Wide fairways and openings to the green, few hazards, or large greens present little or no difficulty to a golfer.

The golf holes illustrated in Figure 9.2 are typical golf holes. Hole A is relatively easy, with few strengths. In contrast, Hole B is a very difficult hole. Note its strengths.

199

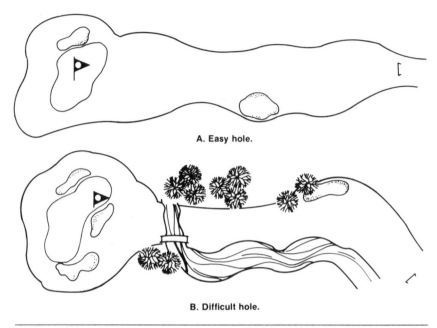

A. Easy hole.

B. Difficult hole.

Figure 9.2. Strengths and weaknesses of a hole are determined by the presence or absence of potential trouble areas.

The abundance of sand traps and the water hazards illustrated in Hole B make it a very strong hole. It's strengths relate to the location of the hazards and the pressures they put on most golfers. Each of these factors (location of hazards, the size and shape of the green, and pin placements) should focus your attention to various aspects of the hole.

Matching Your Strengths to the Hole's Weaknesses

Once you have identified your individual tendencies through practice and play and have identified the strengths and weaknesses of the hole, you are ready to attack. The final step is to learn to score. Matching your strengths to the hole's weaknesses is playing "percentage golf."

CLUB SELECTION

Having selected the desired route and target area, your next step is to choose the club. The appropriate club selection depends on the lie of the ball, the desired trajectory, and the distance needed.

The lie of the ball can be considered "good" or "bad." A lie that is not below the surface of the ground (in a divot, buried in the sand, or in the high grass) is considered a "good" lie. The better the lie, the greater number of club selection and shot choices.

The trajectory is the height or loft desired on the ball flight. As the club numbers increase, the trajectory increases, thus providing you with a range of choices. You can also vary the angle of approach on the ball in order to change the trajectory of the ball flight by altering the ball position.

The distance needed is determined by yardage markers on the course, knowledge of the course from playing, or visual perception of the distance acquired through practice. Your choice of club for a given distance comes from practice and knowing how far you hit each club, and your ability to vary the pace and length of your swing.

It is the mix of lie, trajectory, and distance that provides tremendous challenges in golf. You must consider all three of these factors in order to execute a desired shot.

COMPOSURE

Many aspects, both physical and psychological, are involved in planning your strategy for any particular hole. Thus far we have focused on your physical abilities and the physical structure of the course design. However, there is another important component—the mental aspect. As with the physical aspects, you must conquer the psychological aspects of playing a round of golf.

Each golf hole can make you feel either composed or anxious. You must analyze the strengths and weaknesses of the hole in terms of both its psychological and physical demands. Consider the following situation. You are standing on the tee of a 355-yard par 4 with a dogleg left. The dogleg is about 210 yards out. The left side is lined with thick foliage. The right side is fairly open, with little trouble. The end of the fairway to the far side of the dogleg is 245 yards. Two of your playing partners have hit. One flew the dogleg and is in the middle of the fairway 100 yards from the green. The other partner is potentially lost in the thick foliage. Your normal ball flight is high with a right curvature. How are you going to play this hole?

Listen to Your Self-Talk

If you are standing there thinking about the partner who successfully drove over the dogleg, and are thinking about trying to "crunch" your tee shot—think again. On this 355-yard hole, distance is not a major factor. Control is the key. It might be better to match your skills with the hole's weakness—an open landing area to the right of the dogleg.

201

Selecting a 3- or 4-wood for greater control off the tee may be more realistic. Know yourself. Don't be tempted by your partners, nor scared by their location in the rough. Plan your own game. Analyze your strengths and their relationship to this hole.

One of the worst mistakes a golfer can make is to try to overplay a hole. If you tend to hit a slight fade, don't suddenly try to create a hook in a tight situation, unless you have successfully practiced altering your ball flight. That's not percentage golf.

The way in which you talk to yourself may be very revealing about the anxiety-provoking nature of each golfing situation. If you are preparing to tee off and are doubting yourself ("Oh no, not another hazard"), or replaying a past hole ("If only I had made that putt on 7"), you may be creating a difficult psychological hole. Similarly, if you focus on the partner who may have already lost a ball, you will be distracted and begin to build negative thoughts.

You must treat the psychologically difficult hole in the same way you treat a physically tough hole. Objectively analyze the strengths and weaknesses of the hole, compared with your own strengths and weaknesses. Match them so that you can capitalize on your strengths. Employ thought-stopping techniques if appropriate, positive visual imagery, and good pre-swing preparation.

When you look down a rather difficult hole, do you imagine yourself conquering the hole, or succumbing to it? Can you use the thought-stopping technique to regain control? If you imagine yourself going out of bounds or landing in a water hazard, say "stop," relax, and say "I'm in control." Then proceed with your regular routine.

Visualization

Some golfers feel themselves become tense and start to rush their shots. If you are anxious, take a little longer over your shots. Look at that putt until the cup grows twice as large and until the path of your putt looks as if it will run down a set of railroad tracks. Stare at the putt if you must, but before you stroke it, see it roll smoothly along the tracks and drop into the hole.

When you look over that hole, can you see the entire plan? Where will your first shot land? What club will you hit? Where will your second shot land? What trajectory will it have? If you doubt your ability to hit a 3-iron (or whatever), say "stop, relax" and then let it happen. See that approach shot. If you are rushing before you hit it, say "stop, relax," back off, and start your routine again. You must be able to capitalize on the good information you have stored after so much practice. Get out of the way of your swing. Analyze your skills, and then let your body execute them.

Visualization and positive rehearsal are keys to good course management. Close your eyes and play out a hole in several different ways. This will allow you to plot your strategy and select the best route. Once you have done that, choose a target and "go for it."

Once you have executed the shot, take a moment to analyze it. If it was a great shot, savor it. Store it away, and replay it. If it was a less-than-perfect shot, replace it. Always remember—"Replace the bad, repeat the good." When you prepare for your next shot, be sure to imagine the perfect shot. Take a practice swing, and feel your body execute the perfect shot. Allow yourself to both feel and see the perfect shot in your imagination. Remember, "winners see what they want to happen, losers see what they fear might happen." You must allow yourself to see and feel what your body can execute.

Target selection is a key to effective mental course management. You must select your goal, then match it with your club and your abilities. Once this "landing area" goal has been chosen, select an intermediate target to help with alignment, then refocus on your ultimate target. Now allow your swing to hit the ball. Don't try to guide the ball, just swing!

Use your mental skills after each shot, in order to learn from it. If it was a good hit, save it. If it was not as good as you desired, replace it in your mind's eye. Then forget it, and go on to the next shot.

Use your powers of visualization and positive rehearsal to build confidence. Remember to use all of the available cues, but don't get distracted by irrelevant ones. For example, the golfer in Figure 9.3 mentioned that he was quite distracted by his own shadow. If that happens to you, you have two positive ways to handle it: try to focus in on the ball and ignore your shadow, or briefly use the shadow to build your confidence. Notice your good posture and setup, and then say "Relax . . . I know I can hit this shot."

Attention Control

Some golfers try to actively manage their attention throughout a round of golf. This is quite difficult when you consider the typical 4 1/2 hour round. Instead, practice controlling your attention only when it counts. There is nothing wrong with letting your mind wander between shots. Stop and smell the flowers, chat with your golfing partners, or just enjoy the day. But before you get ready for your next shot, regain your attention, and focus in on your golf game. There is an old saying in golf—"focus in, don't block out." When it is time to strike the ball, you had better be concentrating on the shot.

One good strategy is to use your preshot routine as a cue to regain your attention. Whenever you set your bag in preparation for a shot—whether you park your cart, your caddy sets the bag on the ground, or you begin to analyze the shot—let that be your cue. Anything goes between shots, but when you begin to approach your next shot, establish a key time that will be your signal to concentrate.

Figure 9.3. Allow your shadow to help you build confidence, not to distract you.

The key to mind management on the course is to know when and how to think. Don't try to snow yourself, just know yourself. Be prepared to use the relaxation techniques discussed, the self-talk control, the attentional strategies, and the anxiety management techniques. Then you will be able to manage your mind, your body, and the golf course itself.

10

LEARNING FROM A ROUND OF GOLF

Each round of golf provides you with an opportunity to learn about your strengths and weaknesses. You must become a good self-analyzer in order to tell what types of problems you may find in your game. If you do not carefully analyze each round, you may spend too much time on skills that are not essential.

SETTING OBJECTIVES FOR PERFORMANCE

Each time you play a round of golf, you should have a specific objective in mind. Are you playing in order to make a number, to win something, or to beat someone? Or are you playing in order to improve your overall game? If you are playing to improve your game, and if you have been working on a specific skill in practice, you may need to make a commitment to "play through" a round or match. For example, if you have always shied away from your 3-iron and selected another club instead, you may decide that for the next month you will hit the 3-iron whenever it is appropriate. You must be willing to take the consequences and use the round as a chance to practice your shot and test your skill.

Most good golfers have a specific objective in mind everytime they play. Perhaps you are working on using a set routine everytime you strike the ball. If that is your objective, you must force yourself to use it everytime. If something distracts you in the middle of your routine, back away and start again. If you are trying to control the tension in your hands by setting up over the ball and then exerting tension 2-3-4-3 in order to find the proper grip, do it every time.

IDENTIFYING STRENGTHS AND WEAKNESSES FROM PLAY

There are several effective ways to identify your strengths and weaknesses after a round of golf. The most effective techniques involve focusing on both the physical and mental aspects of your play. You must consciously know what you have done, and what you thought or felt while you did it.

Physical Aspects of Play

It is important to know what happens to the ball when you strike it. You should keep track of all of the common errors.

- Alignment errors.
- Path errors: push or pull.
- Clubface errors: draw/hook or fade/slice.
- Club selection errors: too short or long for target.

These physical errors are all easily identifiable, and probably well known to you. You see them as a result of your swing, or your friends may tell you about them.

Mental Aspects of Play

The errors or strengths that result from the psychological aspects are not as easily observed. You cannot see them per se, and no one else can tell you about them. But these mental aspects are equally important in determining the effectiveness of your swing.

You must know your mind as well as your body. When you swing, are you distracted, rushed, tense, or unable to concentrate? Think about these aspects after each shot. Determine what happened to the flight of the ball and the flight of your mind.

Most good golfers keep track of the mental aspects of their games. They typically consider the following common mental errors.

- Attention control—good direction or distraction.
- Quality of thoughts—negative or positive.
- Tension control—over/under arouse, grip pressure, etc.

Using a Scorecard

One useful technique is to make a note of every shot you hit. You may wish to do this during a round of golf, or record your shots and feelings immediately after the round. This is quite similar to the basketball player who plots the position from which each shot is taken and the results of the shot. By keeping track of each club selection and the resultant performance, you will be better able to direct your practice.

206

Analyze each shot taken and the physical and mental aspects associated with it. For example, Tony kept track of a round of golf at Glenhill Country Club. Each shot was analyzed in terms of the physical characteristics of the ball flight, and the mental characteristics of the golfer. If Tony was in complete control, a "CC" was noted. If excess tension occurred and the ball was sliced, two notations were made s/t (slice/tension).

Tony kept track of both physical characteristics and mental characteristics displayed during the round. A golf scorecard for recording the feelings and results of each shot is very useful (Table 10.1).

The analysis of Tony's golf round provided on the scorecard should direct Tony's practice toward improving tension control and alignment. In addition, the numerous instances of negative thinking must be remedied in order to make Tony a self-enhancer rather than a self-defeater.

After Tony's round, he was asked what clubs were used most often when he practiced. Tony commented that the driver and 5-iron were the most often practiced. Do these match the needs demonstrated by the chart? No! Does your practice match your weaknesses, or do you practice your strengths?

Many golfers are truly " ball beaters." They hit many practice balls during the week, but seldom do they really practice. It may be helpful to force yourself to practice your weakest shots. For example, when college players or teams practice, they often set aside a portion of every practice when each player must practice his or her weakest skill. If everyone on the tee spends the middle of practice on something they do not like, then there is no ego involvement. Everyone likes to see their balls go flying, but you need to see the dubbed ones and then correct them.

Plotting a Round

Another good technique is to take a diagram of each hole on the golf course and plot the flight of the ball on that diagram. Many individuals learn more quickly from a picture than from a chart. By plotting or drawing each shot, you may learn to detect your strengths and weaknesses and to practice good course management skills.

Start by taking a diagram of several holes. Each time you hit a shot, indicate your intended target area, draw the actual flight of the ball, and make a note of mental aspects. Look at the example of Tony's play (Figure 10.1). Notice that on the fourth hole, the drive was hit to the left of target and slightly under the desired distance. In addition, the mental attitude was negative. After that first poor shot, notice that no routine was used. What happened on the second shot? Excess

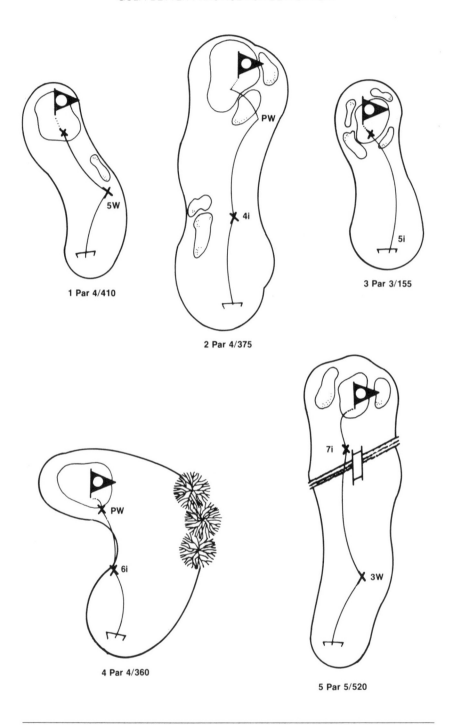

1 Par 4/410

2 Par 4/375

3 Par 3/155

4 Par 4/360

5 Par 5/520

Figure 10.1. Charting a round.

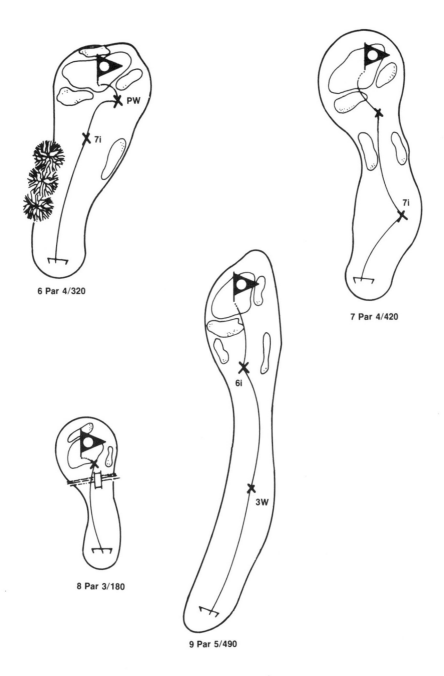

6 Par 4/320

7 Par 4/420

8 Par 3/180

9 Par 5/490

Figure 10.1. Continued

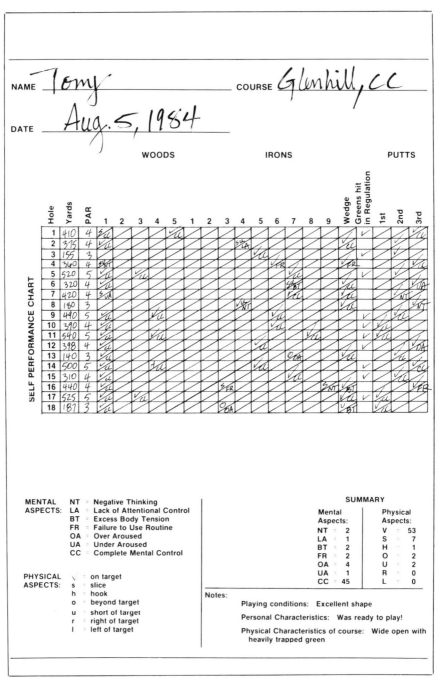

TABLE 10.1 A golf score card to record feelings and results of each shot.

tension was detected and attention was distracted, so the ball landed short of the target. Look at the par 3 eighteenth hole. Remember our discussion of the probability of hitting the ball short on a par three? Tony certainly did that with his 4-iron selection.

A careful visual analysis of your shots may help you analyze your strengths and weaknesses. Record each shot taken for your eighteen-hole round. Each hole should be diagrammed to match the actual course. Doglegs, bunkers, and hazards should all be depicted if effective practice is to result.

Plotting your round of golf may be a much more suitable preference for you. Whether you choose to plot or chart your rounds does not matter, but you must be willing to carefully analyze your play. Take the time to do it. It is not all that difficult, and it will greatly improve your ability to determine your practice needs.

Interpersonal Reactions Within a Round of Golf
Many golfers are influenced by extraneous factors during their round of golf. Do other golfers bother you? Do you play better with certain partners than with others? Does a talkative member in your foursome distract you? You must be aware of these types of mental distractions as well as those that you control more directly.

You may also wish to keep track of your performance depending on when you hit. If you have the honors and tee off first, do you generally drive very well? Or are you better able to concentrate if everyone else has already hit? Do you do better if your playing partner is in trouble, figuring you can relax? Or do you hit well when you have someone else's ball to aim at far down the fairway?

If you are put off by such personal distractions, you must learn to deal with them. You can practice in these situations, using coping and self-talk strategies to help you. It is very important to know what distracts you and to learn to deal with it.

Characteristics of the Course
As you plot or diagram your round, be sure to note any special environmental conditions that may influence you. Do you drive best when there is a wide open fairway, or a tight one? Some golfers concentrate much better on tight holes and consequently play much better. When you see an O.B. (out of bounds) on the right, do you focus on the O.B., or on the 35-yard-wide fairway?

When you have a very tight pin placement, are you able to aim for the most advantageous location, or do you try to overplay your skills? Do you take unnecessary gambles?

Most of the distractions previously listed can be overcome by smart course management and careful shot selection. The importance of identifying a landing area that matches your skills must

211

be emphasized. As part of your routine, you should know how you react to different elements and be able to cope with them.

SETTING SPECIFIC GOALS

Once you have determined your relative strengths and weakneses you are ready to structure practices to improve your performance. You can begin to plan for the future.

The most important aspect of being able to improve your golf game is to know where you are today, and where you hope to go. Unless you were born with an incredible amount of raw talent, your progress toward better golf will require a great deal of work. You must know yourself. Review the chart or plot of your last round. Which skills were executed as planned, and which skills need more practice? Identify your strengths and weaknesses and list them from the best to the worst.

Setting goals for practice and play is a key to maximizing the effects of your practice. You must know where you are and where you are going. There are several things you must consider in order to establish your goal-setting program:

- Identify your strengths.
- List the skills you need to improve.
- Define your goals.
- Plan how you will work to meet your goals.
- Execute your plan.
- Evaluate your progress toward your plan.

Establishing Goals

When you establish goals, be sure that they are realistic and meaningful. One good way to check your goals is to test them by the ABCDs of goal setting.

ABCDs of Goal Setting:
- Achievable
- Believable
- Controllable
- Desirable

An achievable goal is one that you can see yourself accomplish. If your goal is to hit a 5-iron 160 yards, you must be able to see and feel yourself accomplish it. It should be within your capabilities, and you must know that with practice you can accomplish it.

Goals must also be believable. They must be worth attaining and accomplishable. A good goal must be within your own value system, and be worth the sacrifice that it may take to attain it. For example, if you are a very weak hitter, it may not be believable to think that you can hit a 5-iron 160 yards if you can only commit yourself to practice one hour per week. However, if you are willing to dedicate four or five hours of concentrated practice time per week, you may be able to attain that goal.

Attainable goals must also be controllable. You can control how much you practice, or how many balls you hit on the practice tee. But you cannot necessarily control whether you win or lose. If your opponent has an outstanding day, you may not be the winner even though you have played well. Set your goals in terms of practice or scores, not in terms of winning.

Finally your goal must be desirable. Your goal must be something you really want to do. You must be willing to work, sweat, and sacrifice in order to accomplish it. There may be many things you think you should want to do, but a good goal is something you feel you must do. You must really want it. You must be able to see it, believe it, control it, measure it, and achieve it.

A good goal must also be measurable. When you set your goal, you should describe it in terms of something you can measure within a specific time frame. You should be able to state "I will hit one-hundred 5-irons, three times a week," not "I will put in some extra time on my 5-iron." Or, "I will be able to hit eight of ten drivers within a 70-yard fairway, at least 180 yards out." Such goals can be achievable, believable, controllable and desirable.

Sample Goal-Setting Program

The key to effective goal setting is to establish a sequence of stages to guarantee success. If your desire is to be a very good golfer, define some targets and progress through them. Master the stroke first, and then move on to sinking the putt.

Remember our friend Tony. Tony had some trouble putting, and therefore decided to establish the following sequence of goals to improve performance on the greens. Notice that the goals form a sequence from present skill to the desired level.

Let's assume Tony has set the following putting goals. In fact, you may have already accomplished the first three of them.

213

Putting Goals

Accomplished Shot		Goal
_____	4-inch putt	sink ten of ten
_____	8-inch putt	sink ten of ten
_____	12-inch putt	sink ten of ten
_____	24-inch putt	sink ten of ten
_____	3-foot putt	sink eight of ten
_____	4-foot putt	sink eight of ten
_____	6-foot putt	ten inside 12 inches
_____	10-foot putt	ten inside 18 inches
_____	20 to 30-foot putt	ten inside 18 inches

This list of goals will produce a great deal of success. Almost anyone can move through the first step: sink ten 4-inch putts! Start there and build confidence because of your competence—at least from 4 inches. Gradually move farther from the hole, add uphill or downhill putts, right or left breaks, etc. But most importantly, provide a progressive order for building your confidence.

The sequence outlined provides two areas for success. Not that the first five steps produce 100% success. The later steps are built on these successes. For example, at 10 feet all putts should stop within 12 inches, from which point you have already mastered the 100% criteria. Confidence is built in because you are competent at 12 inches—and you know it.

11

RULES AND ETIQUETTE

The rules of golf have a long history, which originated with the Royal and Ancient Golf Association of Scotland. In the United States, the United States Golf Association (USGA) is the counterpart to the Royal and Ancient. The game, which has a rich heritage, has historically been known as a "gentleman's" game. Individual golfers have always been responsible for their own play and conduct on the course, for knowledge and application of the rules and etiquette during play.

The rules provide the framework for direction and order in the game.The more knowledgeable you become about the rules, the greater your advantages. The rules are not intended to hinder the game, but to enhance it. Unfortunately, because many individuals tend to be intimidated by the rules and do not learn the appropriate rule applications, they are often penalized by needless infractions.

Situations on the golf course may be separated into three general categories: actions of players preparing to strike the ball, conditions surrounding the ball at rest, and course conditions independent of the player's control.

The rules to be discussed in this section will be confined to those that are most commonly encountered during play. This is not to suggest by omission that other rules are less important, only that they are less likely to occur during regular play.

Course situations governed by the rules are categorized according to the penalties which may be incurred: 0, 1, or 2 strokes, and disqualification. Situations will be defined and the possible options available to a player will be discussed. It is important to note that all options or alternatives for play may not be appropriate for a player because of other circumstances surrounding the shot or situation.

No penalty stroke is assessed if your ball comes to rest in the following locations.

- Casual water—Water that is on the course as a result of rain or watering systems.

- Ground under repair—Areas on the course under construction or repair which may or may not be marked by a sign or white paint.

- Staked trees—Marked trees on the course that are being protected for growth.

- Sprinkler Heads—Part of the watering system found in the fairway and around the greens.

- Hole made by burrowing animal—Hole made by burrowing animals found on the course (moles, snakes, ants, etc.).

Option for the above situations—The player may hit the ball as it lies, or lift and drop the ball at the nearest point of relief which is no nearer the hole.

Provisional ball—A ball played when the original ball is thought to have landed out of bounds or to have been lost outside a water hazard. If the original ball is found, the provisional ball must be removed from play.

Alternate ball—A second ball played when a question arises concerning the interpretation of a rule or situation. Prior to playing the alternate ball, the player must state which ball will count after a ruling is obtained. If the original ball was the correct way of playing, the alternate ball does not count. If it is not stated prior to playing the two balls, the ball with the higher score counts.

A one-stroke penalty is assessed if any of the following situations occur.

- Lost ball—A ball which cannot be found within a five-minute period of searching. A ball cannot be deemed lost without searching for it first.

  Option—The player must drop another ball at the point nearest to where the original ball was hit from (or re-tee on the tee).

- Out of bounds—Denoted by white stakes placed at the outer perimeter of a golf course, unless otherwise stated on the scorecard. Out of bounds may exist within the confines of a course when deemed necessary for safety, and when designated by white stakes. A visual or string line between the inner edges of adjacent white stakes denotes the out of bounds. If any portion of the ball lies in bounds, it is in play.

  Option—The player must drop a ball (or re-tee on the tee) at the point nearest to where the original ball was hit from.

- Direct hazard—Water which runs across the fairway and has been defined as a hazard. It is usually marked by yellow stakes. Where not marked, the water defines the hazard line (Figure 11.1).

  Options—The player may go back to the point where the ball was originally played and drop the ball.
  Keeping the point where the ball last crossed the margin of the hazard between the player and the pin, the player may go back as far as desired and drop the ball.

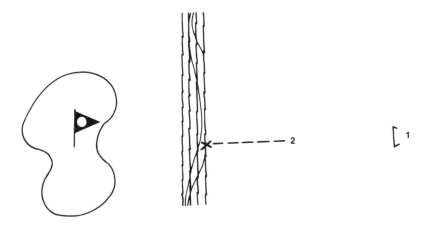

Figure 11.1. Direct hazard options. Example of a ball played off the tee. (x= point where ball last crossed the margin of the hazard.)

217

- Lateral hazard—Water which runs parallel to play and is defined as a hazard. It is usually marked by red stakes. If not marked, the water defines the hazard line (Figure 11.2).

  Options— The player may go back to the nearest point where the ball was originally played and drop the ball.

  The player may drop the ball within two club lengths of the point where the ball last crossed the margin of the hazard—no nearer the hole.

  The player may drop the ball on the opposite side of the hazard from the point the ball last crossed the margin of the hazard—no nearer the hole. Keeping the point that is opposite the entry between the player and the green, the ball may be dropped at any point on the extension of that line.

- Unplayable lie—A ball considered by the player to be in a position that makes it difficult or unsafe for the player to swing. The player is the sole determiner of an unplayable lie. An unplayable lie may be declared at any time except when in a water hazard (Figure 11.3).

  Options— The player may return to the point from where the ball was originally hit and drop the ball.

  The player may drop within two club lengths in any direction no nearer the hole from the point of the unplayable lie. If the ball is in a trap, it must remain in the trap with this option.

  The player may go back as far as desired, keeping the unplayable point between the player and the pin, and drop the ball.

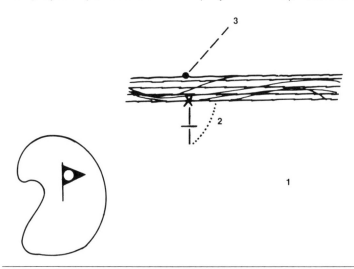

Figure 11.2. Lateral hazard options. Example of a fairway shot hit into the hazard. (x = point where the ball last crossed the margin of the hazard.)

- Ball moved out of position—A ball caused by a player to move out of its original position prior to striking. This can occur when taking the address position, clearing debris from around the ball, or while looking for the ball.

  Option—The ball must be replaced to its original position.

- Whiffing—An attempt to hit the ball in which no contact is made.

  Option—Try again!

A two-stroke penalty is assessed if any of the following situations occur.

- Grounding the club in a hazard—Touching the ground with the club while preparing to strike the ball or in the process of the backswing.

- Wrong Ball—Hitting a ball other than the player's own.

  Option—If a player discovers the wrong ball has been hit during the course of play on a hole, he or she must rectify the error prior to teeing off on the next hole. The original ball is played and only the strokes incurred with the wrong ball are discounted. The strokes made with the original ball are counted and the 2-stroke penalty is assessed.

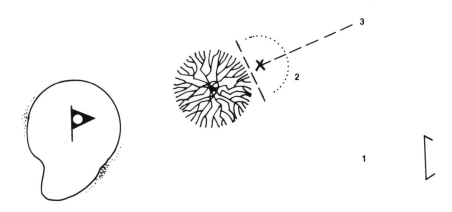

Figure 11.3. Unplayable lie options. Example of a ball behind a tree. (x = the ball.)

- Hitting an unattended flagstick while putting on the green—A pin not removed and hit from the green. When putting on the green, the player must request the flag to be attended or removed from the hole. A flagstick placed on the green and then struck by a putt results in penalty.

  Option—The ball is played from the point where it comes to rest.

- Hitting a ball on the green while putting—Hitting another player's ball while putting. Any ball that is potentially in the path of a ball to be putted should be requested to be marked.

  Option—An opponent's ball that was struck while putting must be replaced to its original spot.

- Requesting Assistance—Only general course knowledge may be requested from opponents or spectators. Any other assistance is illegal.

Disqualification results when any of the following occur.
- Hitting the wrong ball and not rectifying the error prior to teeing off on the next tee.

- Assigning a lower score to a hole than actually obtained, and signing the incorrect scorecard.

The rules are not always as straightforward as they appear. As a result, interpretations by the USGA are requested and often necessary during competition. The current four volumes of *Rules Decisions* are constantly referred to by USGA committees and rules personnel at tournaments. Though these volumes may seem intimidating, they are available in order to clarify the specific application of the rules.

PLAYING BY THE USGA RULES

It is important for each golfer to learn the basic rules and options presented here. The rules can be fun to learn and to share with golfing friends. More important, knowledge of the rules can improve your game.

In the previous chapters, you have read about the importance of mental composure on the course. Consider the following situations and options for play in which knowledge of the rules enables the player to remain composed and possibly save strokes.

Situation

1. A 40-yard wedge shot over a bunker to the green is missed. The ball is buried under a high lip on the green side of the trap.
- Play the shot as it lies. This is a gallant thought, but a very low percentage shot. The potential for wasting strokes is great. The ball could be buried even more.
- Unplayable lie and dropping in the trap. This is the more practical choice. The percentage for executing the sand shot is far greater than the miracle dislodging of a shot buried under the lip (one-stroke penalty).
- Unplayable lie and dropping out of the trap. This option provides the highest potential for execution. This shot is usually practiced more than the sand shot and therefore considered easier for most people. However, it is the one least chosen because people don't know that the ball can be dropped from the trap at the point where the ball was originally played.

2. The course is crowded. Two groups are waiting on the tee. A tee shot is hit into thick woods.
- Search for the ball. This is a "must" by the rules. The player is allowed five minutes to search. If the ball cannot be found, the player must return to the tee and play another ball.
- Hit a provisional ball from the tee. This is the best choice. The player is required to look for the original ball, and if it is found, to take the provisional ball out of play. If it is not found, having hit the provisional ball saves time rather than going back to the tee and slowing up play. Also, it is less stressful to the player and more appreciated by those waiting to play (one-stroke penalty).

3. The hole is 380 yards with a dogleg right. A 200-yard tee shot is hit into a lateral water hazard on the right side of the fairway. The dogleg bends at the hazard. Large oak trees are only on the fairway side of the hazard where the ball crossed into the hazard.
- Replay the ball from the tee. This option is always open. However, in this case, the player loses 200 yards plus the one-stroke penalty.
- Drop the ball on the left side of the hazard. To go toward the green requires a low slice from the heavy rough through the trees. The player's highest percentage strategy is to take the penalty and chip safely into the fairway (one-stroke penalty).
- Drop the ball on the right side of the hazard. From the left side of the hazard, the oak trees are not a factor in the shot. The player has an open shot to the green. This option is least chosen yet often the best. Players fail to take the time to check out the other side of the hazard, even though it may provide the best shot (one-stroke penalty).

221

To learn the rules requires some time and study. Everyone should be familiar with the basic rules and options stated in this chapter. Again, it is suggested that you buy a *USGA Rule Book* to carry in your golf bag. The index is organized by definitions and situations that occur on the course. This allows for a quick and easy reference. Whenever there is any doubt, refer to the rule book. This saves time and unnecessary penalties.

As a player, it is your reponsibility to know the rules and to play by them. Unfortunately, not all golfers play by the rules. This may be from ignorance of or a desire not to acknowledge the rules. How are you going to handle a situation in which you are playing by the rules and your companions are not? Consider the following alternatives.

- Inform them of the rule infraction.
- Share the rule book.
- Assess the penalty.
- Ignore them and play your game.

The decision is not an easy one for any player. You must determine for yourself the importance and nature of the situation.

Competition

When playing in competition, the USGA rules govern. Therefore any rule infraction is subject to penalty, as previously described, and options for play are determined. As a competitor you must play by the rules. If you witness a rule infraction, it is your responsibility at that time to acknowledge it to the player involved. Then if there is any question, it can be resolved or assistance can be obtained at that time or prior to signing the scorecard at the end of the round. Remember, as a competitor your responsibility is to acknowledge the rule infraction, not to provide the rules decision. The player or committee take that responsibility.

Social or Recreation

In social or recreational games, many golfers who know the rules choose not to be as stringent in their enforcement. The actual score of the round may be secondary to the enjoyment of playing with companions. When you play in this situation, accept this approach, allow your companions their choice of play and determine what is best for you. If "modified" rules can be determined at the start of play, potential conflicts or frustrations due to different objectives or goals while playing can be resolved before they occur.

When in a social or recreational setting, you can continue to play by the USGA rules even when your companions choose not to. You are responsible for your own play. Remember, knowing the rules is an "extra club" in your golf bag, not a police badge.

A golf rules examination is presented in the appendix. Directions and answers are provided. The answers refer you to the rule and option for each question. This test is quite thorough. It will give you an opportunity to challenge yourself on the rules and an opportunity to become more familiar with the rule book.

ETIQUETTE

Golf etiquette refers to the conduct of the players during play and generally falls into four categories.

- The courtesies players extend to each other.
- Slow play.
- Awareness of safety factors.
- Consideration or course maintenance during play.

As a player, you should learn the etiquette of play. Through both the knowledge of rules and etiquette, the game is controlled by the individual players. It helps you and others to enjoy the game more fully by acknowledging courtesies to other players and by reducing slow play, opportunities for injury, and unnecessary damage to the course.

Courtesies
When playing golf, think of the Golden Rule: "Do unto others as you would have them do unto you." Extend the same courtesies to other players that you would like extended to you. Many players are easily distracted by noise or movement around them. This may cause breaks in concentration, unnecessary frustrations, and general irritations within the group. Try to be aware of individual responses. The following etiquette suggestions should provide you with some player courtesies that will be beneficial to you and others.

- Avoid talking within hearing range of players who are hitting.
- Avoid moving within visual range of players who are hitting.
- Allow players who have the "honor" to hit first on the tee.
- Allow the person farthest from the hole to hit first.
- Avoid any unnecessary noise (jingling change, rattling clubs, etc.) while a player is hitting.
- Be ready to mark your ball on the green when it interferes with play.
- Acknowledge the good play of others.

Slow Play
All players need to become more aware of how they can avoid slow play. It is not necessary for you to rush shots and run around the course, but you need to know how to maintain the pace of play

without unnecessary frustration. The following etiquette suggestions should provide you with some guidelines for reducing slow play.

- Be ready to hit when your turn comes.
- Keep a constant pace in moving from shot to shot.
- Save long conversations with your playing partners until after the round.
- Stay up with course play. Never drop more than one hole behind the group in front of you.
- When on the tee, be ready to hit when the group in front has completed its second shots or is safely out of your group's distance.
- Avoid excessive practice swings.
- Record your score for the previous hole while on the next tee.
- Place your golf bag (or cart) at the point off the green nearest the next tee.
- When your group is playing slower than the group behind, allow them to play through.
- When your group has reached the green on a par 3, allow the group behind you to hit up to the green.
- Hit only one shot onto the green. Save your practice for the designated areas.

Safety Factors

A golf club and ball can be lethal when carelessly used. Injuries can occur if proper safety precautions are ignored. Many unsuspecting players have incurred such major injuries as loss of vision, concussions, fractures, and contusions from a lack of safety etiquette by others. The following etiquette considerations should be firmly entrenched in all players.

- Yell "fore" when the ball is in flight if anyone is in danger. It's better to be safe!
- Stand behind, or behind and to the side, of players who are hitting in your group.
- Do not walk behind or too close to players who are swinging.
- Do not swing the club in a group of people.
- When swinging, always swing away from people.
- Do not use people as targets when hitting.
- Do not hit if there is any possibility that the group in front may be hit.
- Do not recklessly throw equipment when angry.
- Periodically, check your equipment for safety. Heads of clubs can get damaged and fly off, and shafts with dents are prone to snap off.
- Place rakes with teeth down in the sand trap after use.

Course Maintenance

Golf courses are expensive to maintain, so help keep the course in good condition. Golfers often become overly excited, angered, or just forgetful and unnecessarily damage the course. You want to enjoy yourself and feel free to be expressive; remember that others want the same benefits! Take time to leave the course in the condition you found it. The following courtesies will enhance your play enjoyment and that of others:

- Replace your divots (and those of others when time permits).
- Repair ball marks on the greens.
- Rake the sand trap after you have hit your shot.
- Do not place your golf bag on the green.
- Walk carefully on the greens to prevent spike marks. (Dragging your feet can damage the green.)
- Whenever possible, avoid using any club other than a putter on the green.

Summary

Not everyone who plays golf will become a Beth Daniel or Tom Watson. But everyone who plays is capable of knowing the basic rules of golf and etiquette of play. The fun of the game is to play the course as it was designed, meeting the challenges that arise. Knowledge of the rules provides you with an "extra club" to handle any situation efficiently, and an appreciation of etiquette makes you an enjoyable partner for everyone.

12

CONDITIONING

By now you have had an opportunity to experience time on the practice tee and the golf course. You have probably found and used muscles you never knew existed. This is not uncommon. Contrary to popular belief, golf is not a sedentary sport!

In this age of motorized golf, the game has become more immersed in recreational and social objectives. Both of these objectives are important in the overall desire to play golf. However, fitness is also important to becoming a better player. Consider the following facts about an eighteen-hole round.

- Endurance. A round of eighteen holes takes 4 to 5 1/2 hours. The course is generally four to five miles long.
- Strength. The golf bag weighs close to 15 pounds.
- Flexibility. The actual swing lasts less than a few seconds, uses the entire body, with close to thirteen moving parts.
- The clubhead is capable of being accelerated in excess of 95 miles per hour.

You must determine for yourself the level of golf performance you wish to obtain. If your aspirations are to be better than average, physical conditioning will improve your golf performance.

Conditioning is as important in golf as in any other sport. Physical and mental fatigue can be detriments to practice and performance quality. Without a fairly high fitness level, it is difficult to practice effectively or to sustain concentration and play during the normal 4 to 5 hour rounds. The game can become exhausting and tense under normal conditions, and especially in competition.

Consider the following questions as they relate to your practice sessions and course play.

- How long can you practice or play before fatigue sets in—mental or physical?
- How effective is your swing when you are fatigued near the end of practice or play?
- How long are you able to sustain attention in practice or play?
- How do you feel after practice or play? Tired? Refreshed? Sore?
- Does your game vary in performance according to the environment you are playing in—flat courses, hilly courses, weather changes, heat, cold, etc.?

There are no right or wrong answers to these questions. The effectiveness of your practice time or course performance cannot be measured in specific quantities of time, but rather in terms of the quality of your practice time.

CONDITIONING PROGRAMS

Conditioning for golf should be both general and specific. Like many other sport skills, the golf swing involves the entire body. Therefore a general overall conditioning program is important. However, because the twisting, rotary action of the golf swing is not commonly used to the same degree in other sports or in our daily activities, conditioning of muscle groups more specific to the action of the golf swing is also needed.

Conditioning programs should be implemented in the off season for best results. However, programs may also be started during the season. It may take a minimum of six to eight weeks to feel the effects of conditioning and longer to notice results in the swing itself.

The results of conditioning are individual and depend on your original level of conditioning and the intensity, frequency, and duration of your exercise program. Extensive conditioning is suggested during the off season, with a less extensive program during the season. In-season participation helps maintain the conditioning effect and helps reduce the potential for muscle soreness and fatigue that may affect practice or play.

General Conditioning

The effectiveness of your conditioning program will depend upon your desire to change your health level. A general conditioning program for golf includes three components: strength, flexibility, and endurance. This type of program provides for overall body conditioning of the larger muscles that are important in most sports skills.

Weight training, both with free weights and equipment such as the Nautilus or Universal machines, has become quite popular. Weight machines may be slightly safer for general use, though all programs should be supervised by a qualified instructor. Individuals less experienced with free weights, or any weight apparatus, should be properly informed of the pros and cons of their use. There are not as many controls with free weights as with commercial machines. Supervision is therefore highly recommended in case the weight is too heavy or balance is lost.

Weight machines are readily available in most high schools and colleges, and in community setting such as health spas, sports clubs, and recreation centers. With proper instruction in their use and establishing of individual program goals, these machines can provide a relatively safe and controlled environment for general conditioning.

Cardiovascular endurance should be combined with muscular endurance to provide for overall conditioning. Jogging, cycling (bike or Exercycle), fast walking, and jumping rope all improve cardiovascular endurance. Muscular endurance can be improved by repeated exercises with varying weights.

Every conditioning program should include flexibility and stretching exercises before and after workouts. These exercises increase and maintain range of motion in the joints and protect against potential injury to the muscles during workouts.

Numerous books are available specific to general conditioning. Several of these are suggested in the references at the end of the book. Therefore, a detailed program will not be presented here. However, the following suggested guidelines are provided.

- Warm up and cool down before and after all exercises.
- Stretch before and after exercise workouts.
- It is better to start with weights that are too light than too heavy.
- Heavier weights increase the number of muscles used.
- Alternate arm-leg or upper-lower body exercises when weight training. This reduces muscle fatigue.
- Regularly implemented workouts provide the best results. Weight training is optimal when done on alternate days to balance frequency, intensity, and duration.
- When combining cardiovascular conditioning with weight training, bicycle riding, swimming, or long distance running (1-3 miles) may be combined with the use of weights.

Many weight and cardiovascular exercise programs are available. The following is an example of one such program designed for strength development. It was used at Illinois State University by Linda Herman and then developed and adapted for general sport use at the University of Illinois by Bob Gajda.

The following strength and development program was outlined to determine the beginning weight level for a weight-training-machine station. This program should be designed and supervised by a qualified professional and include these steps:

- Determine your maximum weight for a single repetition for each exercise (trial and error method).
- Determine 50% of your maximum (step 1).
- Breathing: exhale during lift, inhale during recovery.

The following six-week progression is provided as an example.

Maximum Pounds for an Exercise

Leg Press: 100 lbs.

Week	Percent per Week	Workout Weight	Repetitions per Set
1	50%	50 lbs.	2 sets of 10
2	70%	70 lbs.	3 sets of 5
3	90%	90 lbs.	2 sets of 5
4	80%	80 lbs.	3 sets of 5
5	70%	70 lbs.	2 sets of 10
6	100%	100 lbs.	2 sets of 3
7	???	???	20

- Redetermine your maximum weight for a single repetition for each exercise to begin the seventh week ("max-out week").
- Begin a new six-week progression (weeks 7-12).

Another type of program that should be considered is designed to develop strength and endurance. This type of program should emphasize lighter weights with a higher number of repetitions. For example, twenty-five to forty repetitions for two sets with lighter weights will work the entire body. Such exercises are designed to increase muscular endurance.

Commercial weight machines and free weights may not always be available to you. This should not deter your desire to become better conditioned. Table 12.1 provides a guide for specific muscle groups to be conditioned, with corresponding stations on the weight machines and alternatives if the machines are not available.

Table 12.1
General Body Conditioning for Golf
(These exercises should be done in this sequence.)

Muscle Group	Weight Machine Station	Free Exercise Alternatives
Hip Extensors (hamstrings)	Leg press—low	Stationary bicycle
Chest (pectoralis)	Bench press	Dumbell flyers
Shoulders (trapezius/deltoids)	Upper arm press	Pushups
Leg Extensors (quadriceps)	Double leg lifts	Stepups on bench or chair
Forearm Extensors (triceps)	Tricep pull or extensions	Pushups
Hip Flexors (quadriceps)	Double leg lifts	Squats (knee bends—1/4 or 1/2)
Forearm Flexors (biceps)	Biceps pull; rowing machine (reverse grip)	Inner tube curl
Hip Extensors	Leg press — high	Stationary bicycle

When conditioning for golf, avoid overdevelopment (using heavy weights with few repetitions) of the upper body muscles such as the pectoralis, trapezius, and deltoid. Bulk in these areas tends to restrict upper body motion and flexibility. However, general conditioning (light weights with increased repetitions) in these areas is highly recommended.

Specific Conditioning for Golf

Arm and leg strength are important in golf for both distance and consistency. The golf swing may not appear as strenuous as some other sport skills, and it is not as strenuous if only taking one or two swings. Yet, muscular endurance and strength are critical to consistent performance of accuracy and distance over extended periods of time without fatigue.

Strengthening the arm muscles provides for greater club control during the swing and for developing acceleration, which is necessary for increasing distance. The following seven exercises were suggested by Don Fauls, an athletic trainer formerly at the University of Florida. They are designed to strengthen specific arm muscles. It is important as you do these exercises to position yourself as illustrated in the figures. A barbell or any 7- to 15-pound weight may be used. Start with the lighter weight and progress to a heavier one. When 15 pounds is reached, decrease the weight and increase the number of repetitions.

231

ARM EXERCISES

Muscles above the elbow:

- Stand with your arm hanging at your side, fully extended, weight in hand, and palm up (Figure 12.1) Flex or bend the elbow slowly to full flexion. Return slowly to full extension. Repeat ten times.

Posterior arm muscles, above the elbow:

- Raise your arm above your shoulder with your elbow bent or flexed, weight in hand. Straighten your arm. In doing this exercise, keep your arm in the illustrated position (Figure 12.2) to make certain that the triceps muscle does the work, not the shoulder. Repeat ten times.

Figure 12.1. Arm flexion from a standing position to strengthen the biceps.

Figure 12.2. Arm extension from an overhead position to strengthen the triceps.

Anterior arm muscles, below the elbow:

- Rest your elbow and lower arm on a chair or table with your wrist extending over the edge of the table, palm up (Figure 12.3). Place the weight in your fingers and roll it into the palm of your hand. Let your knuckles go toward the ground, then toward the sky (beyond the starting position). Repeat ten times.

Figure 12.3. Finger and wrist flexion.

233

Posterior arm muscles, below the elbow:

- Rest your elbow and lower arm on a chair or table with the weight in your hand, palm facing down (Figure 12.4). Let your knuckles go toward the ground, then toward the sky past the starting position. Repeat ten times.

Figure 12.4. Wrist extension.

Rotator muscles of the wrist and elbow:

• Rest your elbow and lower arm on a chair or table, palm facing up (Figure 12.5). Hold the weight firmly in the palm of your hand. Turn your hand over so that your palm faces the floor. Return to the starting position. Repeat ten times.

Figure 12.5. Rotation of the wrist.

235

- Rest your elbow and lower arm on a chair or table, thumb up (Figure 12.6). Let your thumb come toward your arm, then away (beyond the starting position). Repeat ten times.

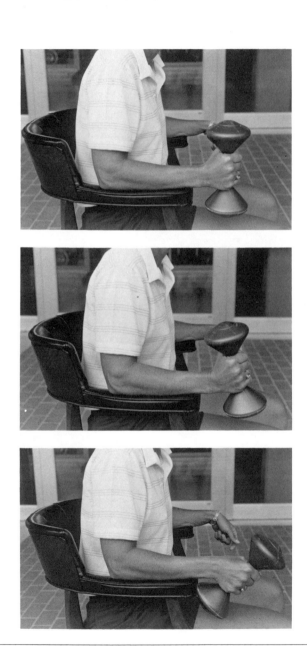

Figure 12.6. Radial deflection.

- Rest your elbow and lower arm on a chair or table, thumb up (Figure 12.7). Let your knuckles go to the left, then the right (beyond the starting position). Repeat ten times.

Figure 12.7. Flexion and extension thumb-up position.

237

These exercises should be done three times a week for optimal results. Two sets of each exercise should be done with each arm. Every week one additional repetition should be added to each exercise until twenty repetitions of each set have been reached. For example, during the fifth week you should do two sets of each exercise, fourteen repetitions per set, for each arm, three times a week. Increase the weight after twenty repetitions have been reached. When the maximum weight level has been attained, decrease the weight and increase the repetitions.

HAND EXERCISES

- Fingertip pushups (regular or modified).
- Squeeze a ball (baseball-size Nerf ball or rubber ball) twenty-five times. Gradually increase by fives. (Both hands.)
- Hold a golf club by your side at the end of the grip. Turn the club counterclockwise with your fingers until fatigued. (Both hands.)
- Hang a weight from a rope tied to a dowel rod. Hold the rod parallel to the ground, each hand on one end of the rod, palms down. Roll the weight up by turning the rod with the hands.

Flexibility is also important to any conditioning program for golfers. It is particularly important to golf because of the twisting, rotary action of the swing. This twisting effect is most often felt in the upper and lower back muscles. These upper and lower back muscles need to be strengthened by a general conditioning program. Additional specific stretching and flexibility exercises should be included, daily when possible and always prior to practice and play. This enhances the efficiency of the back muscles during the backswing and forward action.

The golf swing requires flexibility in the back, hamstrings, and hips. The following exercises are recommended for back flexibility. Each exercise position should be held for a minimum of 15 seconds. The longer you can hold the stretch, the more beneficial it will be. However, you do not want to hold it to the point of pain. Begin by holding the stretch for a few seconds and work up to fifteen seconds. Then relax and return to the starting position. Repeat each exercise three times. These exercises should be done with slow, sustained movement rather than forceful bouncing. A stretched or tight feeling is desired. If any pain occurs, however, that is the body's sign to stop, indicating that you have stretched too far.

BACK FLEXIBILITY EXERCISES

- Stand with your feet together, knees slightly bent (Figure 12.8). Stretch your arms above the head, raising to your toes. Slowly lower your heels and bend from your waist. Hang relaxed (Figure 12.8), allowing the weight of your upper body and gravity to stretch your lower back.

Figure 12.8. Gravity hang.

- Sit on the floor or a mat with your feet together (Figure 12.9). Slowly bend from your waist and try to touch your chest to your feet.

Figure 12.9. Chest touch.

- Sit on the floor with your legs extended. Bend your right leg at the knee, crossing it over your left leg and placing your foot flat on the floor (both hips remain in their original position). Turn your upper body to the left (Figure 12.10). Extend your left arm behind your back. Turn your head to the left, looking over your shoulder. Repeat for the right side.

Figure 12.10. Cross sit position.

- Place your feet six inches from a wall with your back to the wall (Figure 12.11). Keeping your feet together, slowly turn to the right, allowing both hands to touch the wall at shoulder height. Try to keep your hips and lower body facing forward. Repeat for left side.

Figure 12.11. Upper body turn.

- Stand erect, with knees slightly bent. Extend both arms above your head and clasp hands so that both palms are facing upward (Figure 12.12). Bend forward from your waist, allowing your upper body to hang. Raise your upper body, with your arms extending over your head. Slowly lower your extended arms below your head to your waist while your head is tilted backward.

Figure 12.12. Neck and shoulder stretch.

243

- With your hands clasped and arms extended above your head, bend your upper body laterally to the left (Figure 12.13). Repeat for right side.

Figure 12.13. Side stretch.

Summary

Conditioning will improve your potential to play better golf. A conditioning program can be fun and beneficial. As with any goal, the desire to improve your fitness level requires a commitment. An irregular or half-hearted effort will prove worthless. You must now determine your present level of fitness and make the commitment. Set specific goals for your conditioning program and work toward accomplishing them.

13

EQUIPMENT SELECTION AND SPECIAL CHARACTERISTICS

As your golf game progresses, you may want to give some consideration to your equipment, present or future. This chapter will provide you with some thoughts and basic information regarding the equipment on the market today.

Golf equipment has both aesthetic and performance designs. For many golfers the club's visual appearance influences their ability to use the equipment. The "different looks" may be seen in Figure 13.1. Notice the variations in the irons. Some have a sharp toe, others a rounded toe, a glossy finish or a dull finish, a standard hosel or an offset hosel. The individual may choose from a wide variety.

It has been suggested that, for many golfers, visual appearance is the most important aspect of selecting a golf club. This assumes that the performance potential for the various makes and models and the performance potential for all golfers are equal. Not true! Let's look at the following descriptions of a few golfers.

- Golfer A—Golf Professional on the LPGA or PGA tour. Strikes five-hundred balls a day in practice and plays eighteen holes a day.
- Golfer B—A golfer with a single-figure handicap, hits three-hundred balls four times a week, and plays eighteen holes three times a week.
- Golfer C—A golfer with a middle-ranged handicap fifteen to twenty, hits one-hundred balls twice a week, and plays eighteen holes twice a week.
- Golfer D—A golfer with a high range handicap (twenty-seven and greater), plays once or twice a week.

From the foregoing descriptions, as well as other available information, we realize that not all golfers perform the same, not all golfers have the same intensity or desire to practice, and golfers play

245

for a variety of reasons. Depending on where you fall on the continuum of practice and play, selecting the best golf club design for your performance needs may enhance your ability to score.

In recent years the golf industry has directed more attention to the performance needs of the middle- to high-handicap golfer. Off-center hits, higher ball trajectory, and more durable ball covers are examples of design changes which provide a greater margin for error.

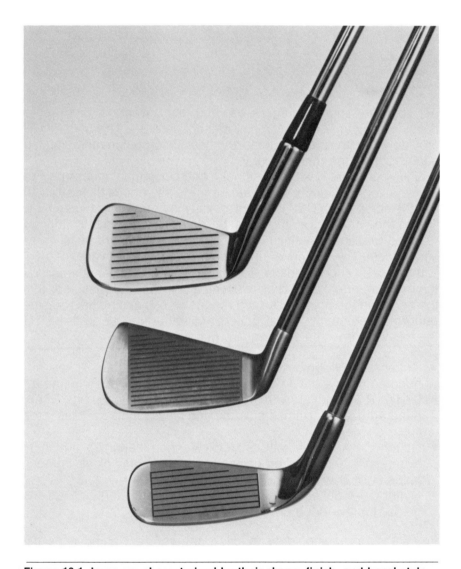

Figure 13.1. Irons are characterized by their shape, finish, and hosel style.

The following section will provide you with some general information on golf equipment. When deciding to purchase equipment you should seek out a knowledgeable individual in your area for advice. If possible, ask for an opportunity to hit shots with different clubs. Demonstration models should be available.

GOLF CLUBS

Woods

Two types of "woods" are on the market today: the traditional and the metal (Figure 13.2). The traditional wood is a solid hardwood head, (e.g. persimmon) or a head made of layered strips of wood glued together (laminated). The choice of persimmon over laminated is a preference made by the individual. There is little indication that a significant performance difference exists between the use of persimmon and laminated woods. The greater difference is found in the cost; persimmon is considerably more expensive because of manufacturer cost in obtaining the rare persimmon.

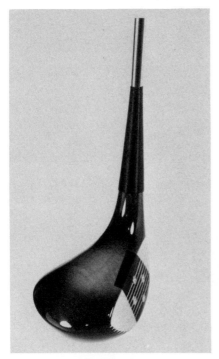
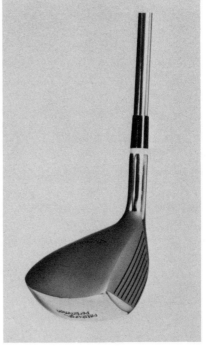

Traditional.   Metal.

Figure 13.2. Two types of woods are available: traditional and metal.

The metal woods have become popular since about 1978. They have been nicknamed the "Pittsburgh Persimmon" by their original manufacturer.

When metal heads are compared with traditional woods, a notable performance difference, in both distance and accuracy favors the metal woods. This difference is due to the club design at the hosel and the hardness of the metal constuciton. The smaller hosel design reduces wind resistance, thereby potentially increasing clubhead acceleration, which can then increase the distance of the drive. The metal construction provides a harder substance from which the ball rebounds and a more equal weight distribution in the head for a wider margin of error.

Irons

There are two basic iron constructions: the traditional or forged iron, and the more recent cast iron. The forged iron is less expensive for the manufacturer to produce. However, with respect to feel and performance for the player, the difference is negligible. The choice then becomes a preference.

Figure 13.3. The offset has the leading edge of the blade back from the hosel.

NEW DESIGNS

Offset Hosel

The traditional iron/wood design has the hosel in line or even with the leading edge. The offset hosel (Figure 13.3) design has the leading edge of the striking surface back from the hosel in varying degrees, depending upon the model. The offset design is relatively new, available since the late 1960s.

The choice of the traditional vs. the offset is a preference in both appearance and performance. Many golfers, of all ability levels, have difficulty adjusting to the offset look, particularly when they have been playing with the traditional hosel for years.

The offset hosel was originally designed to help the middle- to high-handicap golfer strike the ball with descent (the hands leading the club at impact). Since that time, this design has become extremely popular for all levels.

Heel-Toe Balance

Heel-toe balance refers to a club design in which there is equal weight distribution in the head of the club between the heel and toe (Figure 13.4). This differs from the traditional design in which the weight distribution in the clubhead lessens as the distance increases from the club's center point (the centroid) toward the heel and toe.

The heel-toe balance provides the golfer with a wider margin for error, which is not possible with the traditional design. In the traditional design, when the ball is struck in either direction (toward the heel or toe) away from the club's center, shot control lessens for both distance and accuracy. The club has a twisting effect with off-center hits, which lessens the stability of the club at the heel or toe. This effect is reduced with the even-weight distribution.

Low Profile

The low profile design (Figure 13.4—the bottom club) places additional weight in the sole or bottom of the club. This lowers the club's center of gravity, which results in the ball flying at a higher trajectory. This design helps individuals who have problems getting the ball airborne.

Sole Design

The sole of the club may be from wide and flat to narrow and sharp (Figure 13.4—top club). When the sole of the club contacts the ground, it bounces. The wider, flat sole reduces the normal digging effect of the club, allowing the golfer to produce less "heavy" of "fat" shots. This design is favored by the middle- to high-handicap golfer. The angled design provides a sharper leading edge for hitting down and through the turf. The angled design is preferred by the professional and low-handicap golfers who have greater arm and clubhead control.

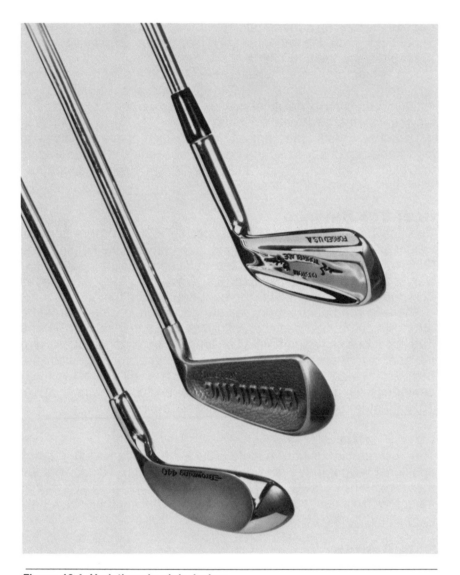

Figure 13.4. Variations in club design.
Top—traditional.
Middle—heel-toe weight distribution.
Bottom—sole weighting.

CHARACTERISTICS OF THE TOTAL GOLF CLUB

Up to this point, the head of the club has been discussed, from the aesthetic appearance to the performance design features. A few other characteristics of the overall club effectiveness also need to be discussed: grip, shaft, weight, and lie. Each of these will be discussed briefly as they relate to club selection.

It is important to understand the contributions that each of the elements of a golf club provides to the club's overall effectiveness. When the time comes for selecting your equipment, seek out a qualified individual to help you bring these elements together.

Grip

Grips are made with a variety of textures. Feel a rubber composition surface and then a leather surface. Can you feel a difference? Or can you distinguish the difference in the feel of two leather surfaces, one rough and one smooth? Do you have a preference—rough, smooth, leather, or rubber? Choosing grip texture is a preference. Different types should be available for you to try.

Grips vary in size, too. The grip size depends on the individual hand size. Figure 13.5 illustrates the recommended grip fit with contrasting grips that are too small and too large. Note the recommended fit—the middle finger of the target hand just touches the palm. Improper grip size could affect hand action. For example, a grip that is too small could cause excessive hand action. The reverse is true of a grip that is too large; it could reduce hand action. Either of these, too large or too small, could be an asset or limitation depending on the individual's needs relative to his or her swing. Comfort is also a consideration in grip size.

Grips with a different design are also available upon request for individuals who have special problems with gripping. This grip design is generally referred to as an arthritic grip and has a wider base that takes pressure off the finger joints.

Time should be taken to be sure the feel and size of the grip are best for you. Remember, this is your only contact with the club. The grip is your sole communication of club feel and awareness during the swing!

Shaft

Many different types of shafts are on the market. In fact, so many are available that for even the most advanced player, it becomes overwhelming to choose one. Shafts are made of a variety of metals and alloys (e.g. graphite, titanium, steel, fiberglass) with different flexibilities, ranging from extra stiff to very flexible, and different

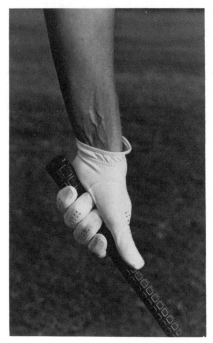 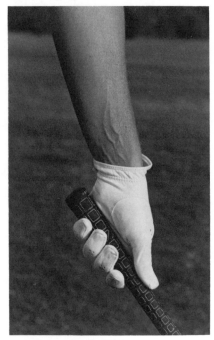

Too small.   Too large.

Proper fit.

Figure 13.5. Grip sizes.

weights, from heavy to light. The various metals and alloys in combination with different flexibilities and weights provide an assortment of feel and performance characteristics from which a golfer may choose.

Flexibility refers to the amount of bending in the shaft, and can vary in bendability as much as a broomstick compared with a garden hose. Stiffness (or flexibility) is relative to each golf manufacturer's standards. Degree of flexibility may be indicated by continuum, be it a series of letters (A, B, C, D, etc.) numbers (1, 2, 3, 4, etc.), or simply names (extra stiff to very flexible).

For the golfer, flexibility may affect directional control and distance. Your individual swing characteristics determine the type of shaft that is best for you. Try swinging a garden hose or jump rope at a target or a golf ball. Your objective is to swing the hose or rope so that it is completely straight or extended when it hits the target of the ball. If you have a smooth, rhythmic swing (a good arm swing), this is an easy task. However, if you swing quite fast and hard and use much body force or hand action, this task is more difficult.

Generally, individuals who are stronger or who have faster swing paces can accommodate a stiffer shaft. Individuals with less speed and force in their swings should consider more flexible shafts. The majority of players fall within the medium stiff and regular shaft flexibility range. Shaft flexibility has no "sex." Both men and women must match their swing characteristics to the flexibility of the shaft. Try different flexibilities to determine which is more effective for your swing timing. In your golf career you may change flexibilities several times depending on your stage of swing development as well as your physical strength.

Weight

Golf club weight may be referred to as swing weight or overall weight. Swing weight refers to the club's weight distribution from the grip to the head. The overall weight on the swing weight scale ranges from 0 to 35 grams. The heel-toe balance of the club is measured as A to E. Most clubs fall within the C-D range, which can be given a corresponding gram weight. The actual weight difference within these ranges is quite small. A dime (.07 ounces) placed on a club represents the difference of one swing weight. This difference is very difficult to distinguish when holding a club. However, swing weight changes of plus two or more can be distinguished. A club with an overall weight that is too light or too heavy is difficult to control during the swing, and this affects distance and accuracy.

253

Lie

The lie of the club is the relationship or the sole of the club to level ground when an individual takes his or her normal address position. Figure 13.6 illustrates three possible club lies: flat, desired, and upright.

Flat.

Desired.

Upright.

Figure 13.6. Club lies.

The desired lie for an individual is one in which the club is level on the ground at address. This provides for maximum on-center ball contact at impact. Note, however, that there may be some slight elevation at the toe and heel with certain sole designs.

A lie that is too flat causes the toe of the club to be elevated. This may produce off-center ball contact toward the heel, and shots that consistently go more right than left with a normal swing (for a right-handed person.)

A lie that is too upright causes the heel of the club to be elevated. This produces off-center hits toward the toe of the club, which tend to go more left than right with a normal swing (for a right-handed person).

An appropriate club lie for your swing, either too flat or upright, can cause a decrease in direction and distance control. Often by correcting the lie of the club, ball flight patterns improve.

Individuals who are relatively tall, have short arms and long legs may need a more upright lie, whereas individuals who are relatively short and have long arms may require a flatter lie. Manufacturers' charts that provide guidelines for club lie as well as the visual guide previously suggested are available.

UTILITY CLUBS

Sand Wedge

Sand wedges have a wide range of possible design combinations: weak to strong lofts, wide to narrow flanges, low to high bounce, and light to heavy weights. The wedge you use could be an asset or a liability in playing the sand shots effectively. The following guidelines may help you select a sand wedge for your particular needs.

The loft of the sand wedge will vary based upon your needs. A very lofted wedge (60^0) adds height to your shots. However, this may reduce your effectiveness on long trap shots or for longer fairway shots from the green. The reverse is true for a less lofted wedge (55^0). A wedge with a loft of 56^0 to 58^0 may provide a more multipurpose use for the majority of golfers.

The flange width is important because it provides resistance for the club in the sand. Similar to the effect on the fairway, the narrow flange digs, whereas the wider sole stays more on the surface of the sand.

The bounce of the wedge is the most important consideration in selecting a wedge. The two wedges in Figure 13.7 illustrate this concept. When the wedge is placed on a flat surface, the amount of bounce may be seen as the height the leading edge is raised from the surface. The wedge on the right has a good bounce, whereas the

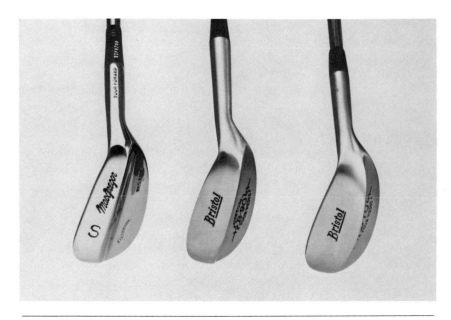

Figure 13.7. Sand wedge design illustrating bounce.

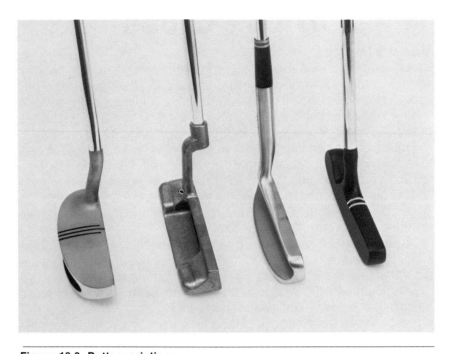

Figure 13.8. Putter variations.

wedge on the far left has the least bounce. The middle wedge is a compromise and could be used as a dual wedge. A wedge with a high degree of bounce is most effective in soft, fluffy (silica) sand, but is much less effective in the coarse, heavy, or wet sand.

The weight of the wedge allows for greater club control. One that is too heavy or too light is relatively ineffective. By design, the club should be slightly heavier than the other clubs in your set because of the wider flange and bounce. As you begin to play different golf courses you will become more aware of the variety of sand textures mentioned in Chapter 3 (coarse, hard sand to soft, fluffy sand). The basic technique will not alter; however, the type of sand wedge used may influence your sand play.

Putters

Hundreds of different style putters of all shapes and sizes are available on the market today (Figure 13.8). The Putter selection is based more on the individual golfer's aesthetic preferences and feel than on equipment performance.

There are several considerations in selecting the best putter for you. The lie should be checked carefully. One that is too flat or upright can cause erratic performances because of off-center hits. The weight of the putter should provide the golfer with feel for both long and short putts. For example, a putter that is too light makes it difficult to feel the distance for long putts because the stroke becomes excessively long.

Putter length is often overlooked. Golfers tend to buy putters that are longer than necessary and choke down to the adequate length for them. This reduces the grip size and associated feel in the hands. For example, a too small grip could cause more active hands than desired.

Putter lengths usually range between 31 and 36 inches. They may be longer or shorter depending on individual needs. When possible, choose the best putter length for you by taking your normal stance, posture, and grip. Note where your hands fall on the putter and measure the length from about one inch above the top hand to the floor. Remember: Choose the putter to accommodate your stroke, not a stroke to accommodate a putter.

BALLS

Golf balls have two types of construction: wound or solid. The wound construction is the traditional ball in which the inner core is surrounded by many layers of rubber binding. The outer cover is made of a balata or Surlyn material. The balata cover is a softer texture which is less durable and is subject to scarring due to mishits, trees, cart paths, etc. However, it lands on the greens more softly than its counterparts, the Surlyn and solid balls. The Surlyn cover is a harder texture, which makes it more durable for the average player.

The solid ball is perhaps the most popular ball on the market. It is very durable and has a high performance for distance.

The newest innovation on the ball market is the colored ball, which may be orange, yellowish-lime, or two-tone (orange/yellowish lime). It is thought that the color enhances the ability to follow the ball in flight and to find it. Ball color is definitely a preference.

Summary

When you go to buy your equipment, shop around. Prices, as well as available club selections, vary considerably from one store to another. Opportunities to try the equipment are very important, particularly when you are not sure of what you want or need. Seek advice from those who know your swing and those who specialize in club fitting. People are eager to sell you equipment and may offer you a good deal. Be sure the equipment fits you and your swing needs. Would you buy an elephant if the price was good, if you had no place to keep him?

APPENDIX: RULES TEST

GOLF RULES EXAMINATION

Directions

This rules examination was designed to help the golfer learn the rules of golf at his own pace with the aid of the rule book. The authors of this exam suggest that you use the following procedure to best learn and remember the rules of golf.

Step 1   Answer the examination questions based upon your current knowledge of the rules of golf.

Step 2   Use the answer sheet to correct your exam and determine which questions you did not answer correctly.

Step 3   With the aid of the rule book, look up the answers to the incorrect responses to determine what the correct ruling should have been according to the given situation. Note: the rule to which you should refer is given after each question and is from the 1982 and 1983 rules books.

Example: Question 1 can be answered by referring to Definition 5b.

Step 4   If you still have difficulty understanding the correct answer after returning to the rule in the rule book, return to the answer sheet and a short statement will explain why the statement was false, or why the choice was the indicated letter.

Although the easiest method is to look up the answer in the answer sheet, we have found that our students and varsity golfers better remember the rules if they have to search for the answers because it requires them to read the rule book in a detailed manner.

We wish you luck and hope that this examination is a helpful tool in learning to play by the rules of golf. It is to your advantage to completely understand the rules because it will prevent you from incurring penalties that will increase your score, and it will allow you to gain every advantage to which you are entitled while playing this great game. We also recommend that you always carry a current rule book in your golf bag so that you have a ready reference when you are faced with the rule interpretation for which you do not have the immediate answer. If you are participating in a tournament and there is an official rules committee, you should seek their help on any matters of controversy.

RULES OF GOLF EXAMINATION

TRUE AND FALSE

___1. A provisional ball is a ball played for a ball that may be lost outside a water hazard or may be out of bounds. (Definition 5b)

___2. "Casual water" is any temporary accumulation of water that is visible before a player takes his stance and that is not a hazard of itself or not in a water hazard. (Definition 8)

___3. Snow and ice are either casual water or loose impediments at the option of the players. (Definition 8)

___4. A large pile of loose dirt or a hole dug in the ground by a greenskeeper is ground under repair even if it is not marked as such. (Definition 13)

___5. Stakes and lines defining ground under repair are considered to be in the area under repair. (Definition 13)

___6. The player or side that plays first from the teeing ground is said to have the "honor." (Definition 16)

___7. When a line on the ground marks out of bounds, the line itself is in bounds. (Definition 21)

___8. When any portion of a ball is out of bounds the ball is out of bounds. (Definition 21)

___9. A stroke is the forward or backward movement of the club made with the intention of fairly striking at and moving the ball. (Definition 31)

___10. If a player starts with ten clubs he may add two more clubs during the round if he does not delay play. (Rule 3-1a)

___11. A player throws his putter after missing a short putt on the ninth green of an eighteen-hold round. He proceeds into the clubhouse, buys a new putter, and plays the final nine holes. This is legal according to the rules of golf. (Rule 3-1b)

___12. If a player does not have the maximum number of clubs in his bag he may borrow a club from an opponent playing on the course. (Rule 3-1b)

___13. If a player discovers during a round that he has one more than a maximum number of clubs, he can declare one club out of play, assess the proper penalty, and continue to play, leaving the illegal club in his bag while completing the round. (Rule 3-3)

___14. Players in match play may by mutual agreement waive a rule of golf. (Rule 4)

___15. Except when otherwise provided for, the penalty for a breach of a rule or local rule is: Match play — loss of hole; stroke play—two strokes. (Rule 5)

___16. If a competitor fails to hole out at any hole before he plays a stroke from the next teeing ground, or in the case of the last hole in the round, before he has left the putting green, he shall be disqualified. (Rule 7-3)

___17. During the play of a hole, a player may not play any practice stroke. (Rule 8-1)

___18. Between the play of two holes, a player shall not play a practice stroke from any hazard, on or to a putting green other than that of the hole last played. (Rule 8-2)

___19. It is illegal to put in a local rule prohibiting a competitor from playing on or to a putting green of the hole last played. (Local Rules, Appendix I)

___20. After completing the first round of a two-round tournament of stroke play, a competitor goes out on the course to play a couple of holes for practice. This is a legal procedure. (Rule 8-3)

___21. A competitor is scheduled to play his first match in a match play tournament. Prior to the start of the match he plays two holes on the course on which the match is scheduled. This is a legal procedure. (Rule 8-3, note 2.)

___22. A player may not ask for or give advice to his opponent during a round of golf. (Rule 9-1 and 2)

___23. A player who has incurred a penalty shall state the fact to his opponent or marker as soon as possible. (Rule 10)

___24. If a dispute occurs in a match play tournament, the claim must be made before the player plays from the teeing ground of the next hole or leaves the last putting green. (Rule 11-1a)

___25. A player in stroke play competition states he scored four on a hole when in fact he scored five. All scorecards are turned in and the tournament is completed. Two days later an official claim is filed. This is an illegal protest. (Rule 11b)

___26. If an official referee has been appointed by the Committee and he makes an incorrect decision, the incorrect decision stands. (Rule 11-2)

___27. In stroke play, if a doubt in procedure or a ruling occurs and no official is present, the competitor shall complete the hole

261

with both the original ball and an alternate ball in a manner that he believes gives him his proper relief. Both scores are recorded and the Committee will rule which ball and score is correct before the competitor signs the card. (Rule 11-5)

__28. For a competitor to use the alternate ball rule, he can announce his decision before, during, or after playing the alternate ball. (Rule 11-5)

__29. A competitor may also use the alternate ball rule during match play competition if no official is present to offer a ruling on a dispute. (Rule 11-5, note 3)

__30. If a player plays out of turn in stroke play, his opponent may require him to replay his shot without penalty. (Rule 12-2b)

__31. In match play if a player plays out of turn, his opponent may require him to replay is shot without penalty. (Rule 12-2a)

__32. If a player needs to play a second shot from the tee after hitting out of bounds, or in the play of a provisional ball, he should do so only after all other players in his group have hit their first ball. (Rule 12-2 and 3)

__33. In stroke play, when a player plays from outside the tee markers, he must replay the shot, counting the original stroke plus the replayed shot and adding the penalty stroke. (Rule 13-2)

__34 In match play, when a player plays from outside the tee markers, his opponent may require him to replay the shot without penalty. (Rule 13-1)

__35. If a player has his ball on a tee and it falls off or he accidentally knocks it off while addressing the ball, the stroke counts. (Rule 14)

__36. The ball shall be played as it lies except as provided for by the rules or local rules. In most cases the Committee will announce local rules prior to the start of play. (Rule 16)

__37. A player may break or bend a branch or twig prior to his taking a stance to improve his intended swing line. (Rule 17-1)

__38. On the teeing ground, a player may press down or cut down the grass prior to hitting his tee shot. (Rule 17-1c)

__39. The player may ground his club in a firm manner in back of the ball to improve his lie prior to striking the ball. (Rule 17-1d)

__40. If a ball is in deep grass, the player may only part enough grass to identify his ball. He is not entitled to part the grass to see the ball prior to playing his shot. (Rule 17-2)

__41. If a ball is in a hazard you may not remove a loose impediment that is also in the hazard. (Rule 18)

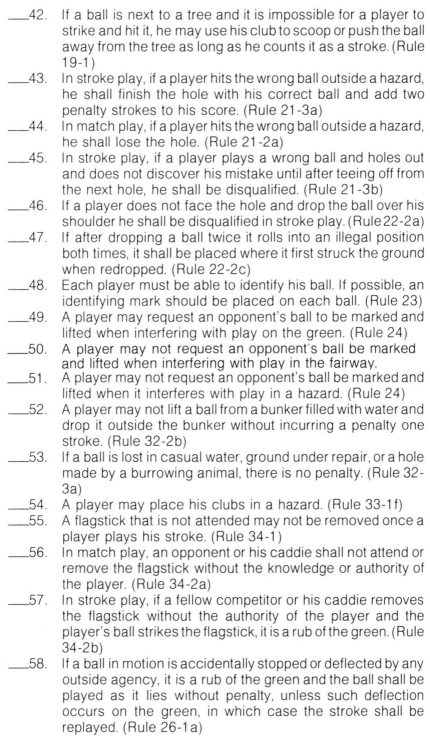

___42. If a ball is next to a tree and it is impossible for a player to strike and hit it, he may use his club to scoop or push the ball away from the tree as long as he counts it as a stroke. (Rule 19-1)

___43. In stroke play, if a player hits the wrong ball outside a hazard, he shall finish the hole with his correct ball and add two penalty strokes to his score. (Rule 21-3a)

___44. In match play, if a player hits the wrong ball outside a hazard, he shall lose the hole. (Rule 21-2a)

___45. In stroke play, if a player plays a wrong ball and holes out and does not discover his mistake until after teeing off from the next hole, he shall be disqualified. (Rule 21-3b)

___46. If a player does not face the hole and drop the ball over his shoulder he shall be disqualified in stroke play. (Rule 22-2a)

___47. If after dropping a ball twice it rolls into an illegal position both times, it shall be placed where it first struck the ground when redropped. (Rule 22-2c)

___48. Each player must be able to identify his ball. If possible, an identifying mark should be placed on each ball. (Rule 23)

___49. A player may request an opponent's ball to be marked and lifted when interfering with play on the green. (Rule 24)

___50. A player may not request an opponent's ball be marked and lifted when interfering with play in the fairway.

___51. A player may not request an opponent's ball be marked and lifted when it interferes with play in a hazard. (Rule 24)

___52. A player may not lift a ball from a bunker filled with water and drop it outside the bunker without incurring a penalty one stroke. (Rule 32-2b)

___53. If a ball is lost in casual water, ground under repair, or a hole made by a burrowing animal, there is no penalty. (Rule 32-3a)

___54. A player may place his clubs in a hazard. (Rule 33-1f)

___55. A flagstick that is not attended may not be removed once a player plays his stroke. (Rule 34-1)

___56. In match play, an opponent or his caddie shall not attend or remove the flagstick without the knowledge or authority of the player. (Rule 34-2a)

___57. In stroke play, if a fellow competitor or his caddie removes the flagstick without the authority of the player and the player's ball strikes the flagstick, it is a rub of the green. (Rule 34-2b)

___58. If a ball in motion is accidentally stopped or deflected by any outside agency, it is a rub of the green and the ball shall be played as it lies without penalty, unless such deflection occurs on the green, in which case the stroke shall be replayed. (Rule 26-1a)

___59. If a player's ball is stopped or deflected by himself, his partner, or either of their caddies or equipment, the competitor shall incur a penalty of two strokes in stroke play and loss of the hole in match play. (Rule 26)

___60. If a player, his partner, or either of their caddies purposely move, touch, or lift a ball, except as provided for in the rules or local rules, the player shall incur a penalty of one stroke. (Rule 27-1c)

___61. If a ball is accidentally moved by a player, his partner, their equipment, or either of their caddies, there is no penalty stroke. (Rule 27-1d)

___62. If a player's ball is touched or moved by an opponent, his caddie, or equipment (except as otherwise provided for in the rules), the opponent shall incur a penalty of one stroke in match play but no penalty is incurred in stroke play for touching or moving a fellow competitor's ball. (Rule 27)

___63. Mud or loose impediments adhering to the ball make a ball unfit for play. (Rule 28)

___64. A player is not the sole judge of whether his ball is unft for play. (Rule 28)

___65. If a ball is lost outside a water hazard or out of bounds, a player shall play his next stroke as near as possible to the spot from which the original stroke was played by him, adding a penalty stroke to his score for the hole. (Rule 29-1a)

___66. A player is the sole judge of whether his ball is unplayable and he may declare a ball unplayable anywhere on the course except in a water hazard. (Rule 29-2a)

___67. If a ball may be lost outside a water hazard or may be out of bounds, a player may play another ball provisionally as near as possible from the spot the original ball was played. (Rule 30-1)

___68. If a player decides to play a provisional ball, he may do so at any time within the five-minute search-time limitation. (Rule 30-1a)

___69. Any movable obstruction may be removed if it interferes with the stance or the area of the intended swing of a player. (Rule 31-1)

___70. A player is entitled to relief from an immovable obstruction if it intervenes with the line of play. (Rule 31-2a)

___71. If a ball lies in or is lost in a lateral water hazard you may drop a ball outside the hazard within two club-lengths of the point where the ball last crossed the margin of the hazard or at a point on the opposite margin of the hazard equidistant from the hole. (Rule 33-3b)

264

___72. For a ball to be deemed holed out it must lie completely below the level of the lip of the hole. (Definition 4)

___73. If a player declares his ball unplayable in a bunker, he must drop the ball in the bunker and add a one-stroke penalty to his score. (Rule 29-2b)

___74. If a player hits his ball into a tree and it lodges in the bark he may deem it unplayable and he may drop a ball as far back from the tree as he wishes as long as he keeps the tree between himself and the hole. (Rule 29-2bii)

___75. A player may not strike at a moving ball unless it is moving in a water hazard or it begins to move after he has begun the backward movement of the club. (Rule 25)

MULTIPLE CHOICE

1. A ball is lost if:
   a. It is not found or identified as his by the player within five minutes after beginning search for it.
   b. The player has put another ball into play under the rules even though he has not looked for the original ball.
   c. The player has played any stroke with a provisional ball from a point beyond where the original ball is likely to be found.
   d. All of the above. (Definition 6)

2. Which of the following are considered to be hazards?
   a. Bare patches and paths.
   b. Grass covered ground within a bunker.
   c. A pond, river, or ditch filled with water.
   d. All of the above. (Definition 14)

3. Which of the following is not loose impediments?
   a. Natural objects not fixed or growing and not adhering to the ball.
   b. Worms and heaps made by them.
   c. Snow and ice.
   d. Sand on the putting green.
   e. Loose soil on the golf course not designated as ground under repair. (Definition 13)

4. An obstruction is anything artificial on the course except:
   a. Roads and paths.
   b. Objects such as fences and stakes defining out of bounds.
   c. Bridges and bridge supports not in a water hazard.
   d. All of the above. (Definition 20)

5. When out of bounds is fixed by stakes or a fence, the out of bounds line is determined by which of the following?
   a. The inside points.
   b. The outside points.
   c. Either of the above, whichever is to the golfer's advantage. (Definition 21)

265

6. Which of the following is not an outside agency?
   a. The competitor in a stroke play.
   b. The referee.
   c. A marker.
   d. A spectator.
   e. All of the above. (Definition 22)
7. The teeing ground is the starting place for the hole to be played. It is a rectangular area, the front and sides defined by the tee markers and extending backwards _____ club lengths. (Definition 33)
   a. One.
   b. Two.
   c. Three
   d. Four.
8. "Through the green" is defined as all areas of the course except:
   a. Teeing ground.
   b. Putting green.
   c. All hazards on the course.
   d. All of the above. (Definition 35)
9. A player shall start a stipulated round of golf with no more than _____ clubs:
   a. Ten.
   b. Twelve.
   c. Fourteen.
   d. Sixteen (Rule 3)
10. In match play, a player loses each hole he plays with more than a maximum number of clubs. The maximum number of holes he can lose under this rule is: _____:
    a. One.
    b. Two.
    c. Three.
    d. No limit. (Rule 3-2)
11. In stroke play, a player is penalized two strokes per hole, for each hole he plays with more than a maximum number of clubs. The maximum number of strokes he is penalized under this rule is:
    a. Two
    b. Four.
    c. Six.
    d. No limit. (Rule 3-2)
12. The penalty for asking for advice during a stroke play is _____ strokes per incident:
    a. One.
    b. Two.

    c. Three.

    d. Disqualification. (Rule 9-2)

13. The penalty for giving advice to your opponent during stroke play is _____ strokes per incident:

    a. One.

    b. Two.

    c. Three

    d. Disqualification. (Rule 9-2)

14. If a player in making a stroke hits the ball twice he shall:

    a. Replay the shot with no penalty.

    b. Replay the shot and add one penalty stroke.

    c. Play the ball and count the stroke plus one penalty stroke, making two strokes in all.

    d. Count the stroke and add two penalty strokes. (Rule 19-2)

15. If a player plays a ball from a hazard and then discovers it was a wrong ball he incurs the following penalty:

    a. No penalty and play correct ball.

    b. Match play—he loses the hole.

    c. Stroke play—it is a one-stroke penalty.

    d. None of the above. (Rule 21-2a and 3a)

16. If a player drops a ball, he shall be given a redrop without penalty:

    a. If it comes to rest against the player's foot after hitting the ground.

    b. If it strikes the player's foot prior to hitting the ground.

    c. If it hits the ground and moves one club length from the original position.

    d. None of the above. (Rule 22-2a)

17. A dropped ball shall be redropped if it rolls:

    a. Into a hazard

    b. Out of bounds.

    c. More than two club lengths from the point where it first struck the ground.

    d. Nearer the hole than its original position.

    e. All of the above.

    f. None of the above. (Rule 22-2c)

18. Under which condition listed below may a player not clean his ball when he is authorized to lift it?

    a. From an unplayable lie.

    b. From an obstruction.

    c. From a water hazard.

    d. On the putting green.

    e. When a lift is not authorized but there is a large piece of mud on the ball. (Rule 23-2)

19. No penalty shall be incurred by a player if a ball in play and at rest has been moved:
    a. Purposely.
    b. After a loose impediment lying within one club length has been touched by the player.
    c. During search by an opponent.
    d. After the player has addressed it. (Rule 27)
20. If a player declares his ball unplayable, he may:
    a. Invoke a stroke and distance penalty.
    b. Drop a ball within two club lengths of the point where the ball lay but not nearer the hole.
    c. Drop a ball behind the point where the ball lay, keeping that point between himself and the hole, with no limits to how far behind that point the ball may be dropped.
    d. All of the above. (Rule 29-2b)
21. A player whose ball lies in a water hazard may:
    a. Touch the ground with his club.
    b. Remove loose impediments.
    c. Touch objects growing in the hazard while addressing the ball.
    d. Touch the water in a water hazard while addressing the ball. (Rule 33-1)
22. A player whose ball lies in a water hazard is not entitled to:
    a. Play the ball from the hazard.
    b. Under a penalty of one stroke drop the ball behind the water hazard, keeping the spot at which the ball last crossed the margin of the hazard between himself and the hole with no limit as to how far back the ball may be dropped.
    c. Play another ball as near as possible to the spot from which the original shot was played under a penalty of one stroke.
    d. Under a penalty of two strokes drop a ball on the other side of the hazard and continue playing. (Rule 33-2)
23. On the putting green it is not permissible to:
    a. Repair ball marks.
    b. Tap down spike marks.
    c. Remove loose impediments.
    d. Clean the ball without asking your opponent for permission. (Rule 35)
24. On the putting green it is permissible to:
    a. Practice putting after you have completed the hole.
    b. Ask your opponent the line of the putt.
    c. Rub your hand on the surface to determine the direction of the grain.
    d. Roll a ball across the surface to determine the speed of the green. (Rule 35)

25. When any part of the ball overhangs the edge of the hole, the owner is allowed:
    a. Five minutes to see if the ball will drop.
    b. To place his shadow on the ball.
    c. A few seconds to see if the ball drops.
    d. To jump up and down with excitement until the ball drops.
    e. To wait until the sun goes down before leaving the green.
       (Rule 35-1i)

Answer Sheet for Rules Examination

1. True.
2. False, before or after.
3. True.
4. True.
5. False. Outside the area.
6. True.
7. False. Line is out of bounds.
8. False. The entire ball must be out of bounds.
9. False. Forward only.
10. True.
11. False. You can replace accidentally broken clubs only.
12. False. You must use only your own clubs.
13. True.
14. False. You may not waive a rule of golf at any time.
15. True.
16. True.
17. True.
18. True.
19. False. Local rules provide for this option.
20. False. This is illegal and results in disqualification.
21. True.
22. True.
23. True.
24. True.
25. False. There is no limit on a protest when incorrect information has been given by a golfer.
26. True.
27. True.
28. False. The competitor must announce this option before playing an alternate ball.
29. False. No alternative ball is provided for in match play. You must settle the dispute before starting the next hole.

30. False. There is no penalty for playing out of turn in stroke play.
31. True.
32. True.
33. False. No penalty stroke is added.
34. True.
35. False. There is no penalty for this action, and you re-tee the ball.
36. True.
37. False. You must leave these objects as they are except in taking a normal stance.
38. True.
39. False. This is considered improving your lie and is illegal.
40. True.
41. True.
42. False. The ball must be struck, not scooped or pushed.
43. True.
44. True.
45. True.
46. False. There is a one-stroke penalty, not disqualification.
47. True.
48. True.
49. True.
50. False. A player may request a ball to be marked anywhere if it interferes with play.
51. False. It may be marked if requested even in a hazard.
52. True.
53. True.
54. True.
55. True.
56. True.
57. True.
58. True.
59. True.
60. True.
61. False. There is a one stroke penalty and the ball shall be replaced.
62. True. Note in either case the ball shall be replaced.
63. False. You can clean your ball only under the special conditions provided for in the rules.
64. True.
65. True.
66. True.
67. True.
68. False. A provisional ball must be played before proceeding forward.
69. True.

70. False. Only if it interferes with his stance or swing.
71. True.
72. True.
73. False. He may also return to the original spot from which the ball was hit.
74. True.
75. True.

Multiple Choice

1. d
2. c
3. e
4. b
5. a
6. a
7. b
8. c
9. c
10. b
11. b
12. b
13. b
14. c
15. a
16. b
17. e
18. e
19. c
20. d
21. c
22. d
23. b
24. a, unless a local rule is in effect to prevent this action.
25. c

SCORING: One point per correct answer

95-100   You're ready for the Pro Tour.
90-95   You're a scratch player with the rules.
80-89   Not bad, but you could stand a brief review.
70-79   You'd better read the rule book again.
60-69   You have a bad slice in the knowledge area that needs correcting.
50-59   You are approaching a mental shank.
Below 50   You are playing another game than golf.

REFERENCES

Anderson, B. *Stretching*. Bolinas, CA: Shelter Publications, 1980.

Croce, P. *Stretching for Athletics*. West Point, NY: Leisure Press, 1984.

Gallon, A.J. *Coaching Ideas and Ideals*. Boston: Houghton Mifflin Company, 1974.

Jacobson, E. *Progressive Relaxation*. Chicago: University of Chicago Press, 1983.

National Golf Foundation. *Golf Lessons*. Palm Beach: National Golf Foundation, 1981.

Owens, D. "Weight Training for Golfers." In J. Cera (Ed.), *NAGWS Guide*. Washington, D.C.: AAHPERD, 1976.

Owens, D. "An Analysis of Amputee Golf Swings." Unpublished Ed.D. dissertation, University of Virginia, 1980.

Owens, D. Golf. In N.J. Dougherty (Ed.), *Physical Education and Sport for Secondary School Students*. Washington, D.C.: AAPHERD, 1983.

Owens, D. (Ed.) *Golf for Special Populations*. New York: Leisure Press, 1984.

Pate, R.R. "Health Fitness." In N.J. Doughterty (Ed.), *Physical Education and Sport for Secondary School Students*. Washington, D.C.: AAHPERD, 1983.

Peterson, J. *Conditioning for a Purpose: How to Get in Shape for Sports and Athletics*. (2nd edition.) West Point, N.Y.: Leisure Press, 1984.

Riley, D. *Strength Training by the Experts*. (2nd edition.) West Point, N.Y.: Leisure Press, 1983.

Rotella, R. and Bunker, L.K. *Mind Mastery for Winning Golf*. Englewood Cliffs, N.J.: Prentice Hall, 1981.

Rowlands, D. and Sherman, D. "Golf Rules Examination." Unpublished, personal communication.

United States Golf Association: *Rules of Golf*. Forest Hills: USGA, 1983.

Solely, C. *How Well Should You Putt*. San Jose: Solely Golf Bureau, 1977.

Thomas, V. Farrell. *Par 3's—the Key to Golfing Success*. Self-published: Salt Lake City, Utah, 1983.

Watson, T. *The Rules of Golf*. New York: Random House, 1980.

Wiren, G. "The Search for the Perfect Teaching Method." *Professional Golfer*, April, 1976.

Wolpa, M. *The Sports Medicine Guide: Treating and Preventing Common Athletic Injuries*. West Point, N.Y.: Leisure Press, 1983.

Zigler, Z. *See You at the Top*. Gretna, LA: Pelican Publishing Co., 1981.